Que® Quick Reference Series

Assembly Language Quick Reference

Allen L. Wyatt, Sr.

Que Corporation
Carmel, Indiana

Assembly Language Quick Reference.
Copyright © 1989 by Que Corporation.

Library of Congress Catalog Number: 88-63831

ISBN 0-88022-428-2

92 91 90 89   4 3 2 1

Interpretation of the printing code: the rightmost
double-digit number is the year of the book's printing;
the rightmost single-digit number, the number of the
book's printing. For example, a printing code of 89-4
shows that the fourth printing of the book occurred in
1989.

Information in this book is based on the instruction sets
of the following Intel microprocessors and numeric
coprocessors:

8086/8088	8087
80286	80287
80386	80387

Que Quick Reference Series

The *Que Quick Reference Series* is a portable resource of essential microcomputer knowledge. Whether you are a new or experienced user, you can rely on the high-quality information contained in these convenient guides.

Drawing on the experience of many of Que's best-selling authors, the *Que Quick Reference Series* helps you easily access important program information. Now it's easy to look up often-used commands and functions for 1-2-3, WordPerfect 5, MS-DOS, dBASE IV, and AutoCAD, as well as programming information for assembly language, C, QuickBASIC 4, and Turbo Pascal.

The *Que Quick Reference Series* also includes these titles:

1-2-3 Quick Reference
C Quick Reference
dBASE IV Quick Reference
DOS and BIOS Functions Quick Reference
Hard Disk Quick Reference
MS-DOS Quick Reference
QuickBASIC Quick Reference
Turbo Pascal Quick Reference
WordPerfect Quick Reference

Publishing Manager

Allen L. Wyatt, Sr.

Editors

Gail S. Burlakoff

Rebecca Whitney

Editorial Assistant

Ann K. Taylor

Trademark Acknowledgments

Que Corporation has made every effort to supply trademark information about company names, products, and services mentioned in this book. The trademark indicated below was derived from various sources. Que Corporation cannot attest to the accuracy of this information.

Intel is a registered trademark of Intel Corporation.

Table of Contents

Introduction

Intel® has created a family of microprocessors that serve as the heart of the majority of microcomputers in use today. Because of the prevalence of microcomputers in computers around the world, programmers need quick reference material that will jog their memory about specific machine instructions.

This book is intended to serve as a guide to the instruction sets for the following Intel microprocessors and numeric coprocessors:

❏   8086/8088 microprocessor

❏   80286 microprocessor

❏   80386 microprocessor

❏   8087 numeric coprocessor

❏   80287 numeric coprocessor

❏   80387 numeric coprocessor

Que Corporation publishes several other books that assembly language programmers may find helpful in their efforts. Among these are

   Using Assembly Language
   DOS Programmer's Reference

The Intel 8086/8088 Microprocessor Family

The popular 8086/8088 microprocessor family from Intel is made up of several different generations of microprocessors. Each generation builds on the previous generation by extending the instruction set and capabilities of the family. The 8086 and 8088, the earliest members of this family, share a common instruction set that forms the base for all successive generations.

Later microprocessors, such as the 80286 and the 80386, understand the same instructions employed in the 8086/8088. This base instruction set is explained in detail in this section. Later in this book, the extensions of this base set for both the 80286 and the 80386 are described.

The Intel 8086/8088 family of instructions can be grouped into six general classifications according to the purpose of the instruction:

> Data transfer
> Arithmetic
> Bit manipulation
> String manipulation
> Control transfer
> Flag and processor control

The individual instructions within each general classification are listed in an overview section titled, for example, "Overview of the 8086/8088." Similar sections are named for each of the other microprocessors.

Throughout this quick reference, each instruction is described in detail. The instructions are arranged by microprocessor (8086/8088, 80286, and 80386) in alphabetical order. The following information is given for each instruction:

Instruction name. This name is based on the standard mnemonic code designed by Intel. The general classification for the instruction also is provided, along with a narrative description of the instruction.

Flags affected. The majority of the instructions change the status of the bits in the flags register. If no flags are affected, then this section is not included for the instruction. The individual flags affected are as follows:

Abbreviation	*Meaning*
OF	Overflow
DF	Direction
IF	Interrupt
TF	Trap

Abbreviation	Meaning
SF	Sign
ZF	Zero
AF	Auxiliary Carry
PF	Parity
CF	Carry

Coding examples. Brief examples of the use of the instruction are given. An example is included only if the instruction name is not used alone; that is, operands or additional instructions are needed to make the instruction work.

Overview of the Intel 8086/8088

The following list shows the complete instruction set for the Intel 8086/8088, arranged in alphabetical order:

AAA	IDIV	JNC
AAD	IMUL	JNE
AAM	IN	JNG
AAS	INC	JNL
ADC	INT	JNLE
ADD	INTO	JNO
AND	IRET	JNP
CALL	JA	JNS
CBW	JAE	JNZ
CLC	JB	JO
CLD	JBE	JP
CLI	JC	JPE
CMC	JCXZ	JPO
CMP	JE	JS
CMPSB	JG	JZ
CMPSW	JGE	LAHF
CWD	JL	LDS
DAA	JLE	LEA
DAS	JMP	LES
DEC	JNA	LOCK
DIV	JNAE	LODSB
ESC	JNB	LODSW
HLT	JNBE	LOOP

LOOPE	PUSHF	SCASB
LOOPNE	RCL	SCASW
LOOPNZ	RCR	SHL
LOOPZ	REP	SHR
MOV	REPE	STC
MOVSB	REPNE	STD
MOVSW	REPNZ	STI
MUL	REPZ	STOSB
NEG	RET	STOSW
NOP	ROL	SUB
NOT	ROR	TEST
OR	SAHF	WAIT
OUT	SAL	XCHG
POP	SAR	XLAT
POPF	SBB	XOR
PUSH		

The following list shows the complete instruction set for the Intel 8086/8088, arranged by general instruction classification. Within each classification, instructions are listed in alphabetical order.

Arithmetic	NEG	*Control-*
AAA	SBB	*transfer*
AAD	SUB	CALL
AAM		INT
AAS	*Bit-manipu-*	INTO
ADC	*lation*	IRET
ADD	AND	JA
CBW	NOT	JAE
CMP	OR	JB
CWD	RCL	JBE
DAA	RCR	JC
DAS	ROL	JCXZ
DEC	ROR	JE
DIV	SAL	JG
IDIV	SAR	JGE
IMUL	SHL	JL
INC	SHR	JLE
MUL	TEST	JMP
	XOR	JNA

JNAE	*Data-*	LOCK
JNB	*transfer*	NOP
JNBE	IN	STC
JNC	LAHF	STD
JNE	LDS	STI
JNG	LEA	WAIT
JNL	LES	
JNLE	MOV	*String-*
JNO	OUT	*manipula-*
JNP	POP	*tion*
JNS	POPF	CMPSB
JNZ	PUSH	CMPSW
JO	PUSHF	LODSB
JP	SAHF	LODSW
JPE	XCHG	MOVSB
JPO	XLAT	MOVSW
JS		REP
JZ	*Flag- and*	REPE
LOOP	*processor-*	REPNE
LOOPE	*control*	REPNZ
LOOPNE	CLC	REPZ
LOOPNZ	CLD	SCASB
LOOPZ	CLI	SCASW
RET	CMC	STOSB
	ESC	STOSW
	HLT	

The following table details the 8086/8088 instructions that affect flags and how those flags are affected. An *X* in a column indicates that the flag is changed by the instruction; a question mark indicates that the flag is undefined after the instruction is executed. Only those instructions that affect flags are included in this table.

Inst	*OF*	*DF*	*IF*	*TF*	*SF*	*ZF*	*AF*	*PF*	*CF*
AAA	?				?	?	X	?	X
AAD	?				X	X	?	X	?
AAM	?				X	X	?	X	?
AAS	?				?	?	X	?	X
ADC	X				X	X	X	X	X
ADD	X				X	X	X	X	X

Inst	*OF*	*DF*	*IF*	*TF*	*SF*	*ZF*	*AF*	*PF*	*CF*
AND	X				X	X	?	X	X
CLC									X
CLD		X							
CLI			X						
CMC									X
CMP	X				X	X	X	X	X
CMPSB	X				X	X	X	X	X
CMPSW	X				X	X	X	X	X
DAA	?				X	X	X	X	X
DAS	?				X	X	X	X	X
DEC	X				X	X	X	X	
DIV	?				?	?	?	?	?
IDIV	?				?	?	?	?	?
IMUL	X				?	?	?	?	X
INC	X				X	X	X	X	
INT			X	X					
IRET	X	X	X	X	X	X	X	X	X*
MUL	X				?	?	?	?	X
NEG	X				X	X	X	X	X
OR	X				X	X	?	X	X
POPF	X	X	X	X	X	X	X	X	X*
RCL	X								X
RCR	X								X
ROL	X								X
SAHF					X	X	X	X	X
SAL	X				X	X	?	X	X
SAR	X				X	X	?	X	X
SBB	X				X	X	X	X	X
SCASB	X				X	X	X	X	X
SCASW	X				X	X	X	X	X
SHL	X				X	X	?	X	X
SHR	X				X	X	?	X	X
STC									X
STD		X							
STI			X						
SUB	X				X	X	X	X	X
TEST	X				X	X	?	X	X
XOR	X				X	X	?	X	X

* Also affects NT and IOPL for the 80286

Instruction Set for the Intel 8086/8088

The instructions presented in this section function as described on the 8086/8088, the 80286, and the 80386.

AAA

Arithmetic

ASCII Adjust for Addition: AAA changes the contents of AL to a valid unpacked decimal number with the high-order nibble zeroed.

Flags affected
AF, CF, OF (undefined), SF (undefined), ZF (undefined), PF (undefined)

AAD

Arithmetic

ASCII Adjust for Division: AAD multiplies the contents of AH by 10, adds the result to the contents of AL, and places the result in AL. The instruction then sets AH to 0. You use this instruction before you divide unpacked decimal numbers.

Flags affected
SF, ZF, PF, OμF (undefined), AF (undefined), CF (undefined)

AAM

Arithmetic

ASCII Adjust for Multiplication: After multiplying two unpacked decimal numbers, you use AAM to correct the result to an unpacked decimal number. For the instruction to work properly, each number multiplied must have had its high-order nibbles set to 0.

Flags affected

SF, ZF, PF, OF (undefined), AF (undefined), CF (undefined)

AAS

Arithmetic

ASCII Adjust for Subtraction: AAS corrects the result of a previous unpacked decimal subtraction so that the value in AL is a true unpacked decimal number.

Flags affected

AF, CF, OF (undefined), SF (undefined), ZF (undefined), PF (undefined)

ADC

Arithmetic

Add with Carry: ADC adds the contents of the source operand to (and stores the result in) the destination operand. If the carry flag is set, the result changes in increments of 1. In this routine the values being added are assumed to be binary.

Flags affected

OF, SF, ZF, AF, PF, CF

Coding examples

```
ADC AX,BX          ; AX=AX+BX+CF
ADC AX,TEMP        ; AX=AX+TEMP+CF
ADC SUM,BX         ; SUM=SUM+BX+CF
ADC CL,10          ; CL=CL+10+CF
ADC AX,TEMP[BX]    ; Indirect address
```

ADD

Arithmetic

Add: ADD adds the contents of the source operand to (and stores the result in) the destination operand. In this routine the values being added are assumed to be binary.

Flags affected
OF, SF, ZF, AF, PF, CF

Coding examples

```
ADD AX,BX          ; AX=AX+BX
ADD AX,TEMP        ; AX=AX+TEMP
ADD SUM,BX         ; SUM=SUM+BX
ADD CL,10          ; CL=CL+10
ADD AX,TEMP[BX]    ; Indirect address
```

AND

Bit-manipulation

Logical AND on Bits: This instruction performs a logical AND of the operands and stores the result in the destination operand. Each bit of the resultant byte or word is set to 1 only if the corresponding bit of each operand is set to 1.

Flags affected
OF, SF, ZF, PF, CF, AF (undefined)

Coding examples

```
AND AX,BX          ;
AND AX,TEMP        ;TEMP must be word
AND SUM,BX         ;SUM must be word
AND CL,00001111b   ;Zero high nibble
AND AX,TEMP[BX]    ;Indirect address
```

CALL

Control-transfer

Perform Subroutine: CALL does the following: (1) pushes offset address of following instruction on the stack; (2) if procedure being called is declared as FAR, pushes segment address of following instruction on the stack; (3) loads IP with the offset address of the procedure being called; and (4) if procedure being called is declared as FAR, loads CS with the segment address of the procedure being called.

Execution then continues at the newly loaded CS:IP address until RET is encountered.

Coding examples

```
CALL WHIZ_BANG     ;
CALL [BX]          ;Subroutine at
                   ;address in [BX]
CALL AX            ;Address in AX
```

CBW

Arithmetic

Convert Byte to Word: CBW converts the byte value in AL to a word value in AX by extending the high-order bit value of AL through all bits of AH.

CLC

Flag- and processor-control

Clear Carry Flag: CLC clears the flags register's carry flag by setting the flag to 0.

Flags affected
CF

CLD

Flag- and processor-control

Clear Direction Flag: CLD clears the direction flag of the flags register by setting the flag to 0.

Flags affected
DF

CLI

Flag- and processor-control

Clear Interrupt Flag: CLI clears the interrupt flag of the flags register by setting the flag to 0. While the interrupt flag is cleared, the CPU recognizes no maskable interrupts.

Flags affected
IF

CMC
Flag- and processor-control

Complement Carry Flag: CMC switches the carry flag of the flags register to the opposite of the flag's current setting.

Flags affected
CF

CMP
Arithmetic

Compare: CMP is considered an arithmetic instruction because the source operand is subtracted from the destination operand. The result, however, is used for setting the flags—it is not stored anywhere. You can use subsequent testing of the flags for program control.

Flags affected
OF, SF, ZF, AF, PF, CF

Coding examples
```
CMP  AX,BX            ;
CMP  AX,TEMP          ;TEMP must be a word
CMP  SUM,BX           ;SUM must be a word
CMP  CL,3             ;Compare to constant
CMP  AX,TEMP[BX]      ;Indirect address
```

CMPSB
String-manipulation

Compare Strings, Byte-for-Byte: CMPSB compares strings, byte-by-byte. DI and SI change in increments or decrements of 1, depending on the setting of the direction flag. Ordinarily, this instruction is used with the REPE, REPNE, REPNZ, or REPZ instructions to repeat the comparison for a maximum of CX number of bytes. Intel lists this command as CMPS, but various assemblers make the byte (CMPSB) and word (CMPSW) distinctions. This instruction affects only the flags; no changes are made to the operands.

Flags affected
OF, SF, ZF, AF, PF, CF

Coding examples
```
CMPSB              ;Compare strings
REPE CMPSB         ;Repeat
```

CMPSW

String-manipulation

Compare Strings, Word-for-Word: CMPSW compares strings, word-for-word. DI and SI change in increments or decrements of 2, depending on the setting of the direction flag. Ordinarily, this instruction is used along with REPE, REPNE, REPNZ, or REPZ instructions to repeat the comparison for a maximum of CX number of words. Intel lists this command as CMPS, but various assemblers make the byte (CMPSB) and word (CMPSW) distinctions. This instruction affects only the flags; no changes are made to the operands.

Flags affected
OF, SF, ZF, AF, PF, CF

Coding examples
```
CMPSW              ;Compare strings
REPE CMPSW         ;Repeat loop
```

CWD

Arithmetic

Convert Word to Doubleword: CWD converts the word value in AX to a double word value in DX:AX by extending the high-order bit value of AX through all bits of DX.

DAA

Arithmetic

Decimal Adjust for Addition: DAA corrects the result (AL) of a previous binary-coded decimal (BCD) addition operation.

Flags affected
SF, ZF, AF, PF, CF, OF (undefined)

DAS

Arithmetic

Decimal Adjust for Subtraction: DAS corrects the result (AL) of a previous binary-coded decimal (BCD) subtraction operation.

Flags affected
SF, ZF, AF, PF, CF, OF (undefined)

DEC

Arithmetic

Decrement: DEC changes, in decrements of 1, the contents of the operand. The operand is assumed to be an unsigned binary value.

Flags affected

OF, SF, ZF, AF, PF

Coding examples

```
DEC AX
DEC SUM
DEC CL
DEC TEMP[SI]
```

DIV

Arithmetic

Divide: If the operand is a byte value, DIV divides the contents of AX by the contents of the operand, then stores the result in AL and the remainder in AH. If the operand is a word value, DIV divides the contents of DX:AX by the contents of the operand, then stores the result in AX and the remainder in DX. This instruction treats numbers as unsigned binary values.

Flags affected

OF (undefined), SF (undefined), ZF (undefined), AF (undefined), PF (undefined), CF (undefined)

Coding examples

```
DIV BX              ;AX=DX:AX/BX
DIV WRDTMP          ;AX=DX:AX/WRDTMP
DIV BYTE_SUM        ;AL=AX/BYTE_SUM
DIV WORD_TBL[BX]    ;Indirect address
```

ESC

Flag- and processor-control

Escape: This instruction provides a means for coprocessors (such as the 8087 or other numeric coprocessors) to access data in the data stream of the microprocessor.

When this instruction is encountered, it causes the
microprocessor to place the operand on the data bus and
perform a NOP internally.

Coding examples

```
ESC  6,TEMP
ESC 15,CL
```

HLT

Flag- and processor-control

Halt: HLT causes the microprocessor to stop execution,
and leaves the CS:IP registers pointing to the instruction following the HLT. This halt condition is termi-
nated only after the system receives an interrupt or the
RESET line is activated.

IDIV

Arithmetic

Integer Divide: If the operand is a byte value, IDIV
divides the contents of AX by the contents of the
operand, then stores the result in AL and the remainder
in AH. If the operand is a word value, IDIV divides the
contents of DX:AX by the contents of the operand, then
stores the result in AX and the remainder in DX. This
instruction treats numbers as signed binary values.

Flags affected

OF (undefined), SF (undefined), ZF (undefined), AF
(undefined), PF (undefined), CF (undefined)

Coding examples

```
IDIV BX                ;AX=DX:AX/BX
IDIV WRDTMP            ;AX=DX:AX/WRDTMP
IDIV BYTE_SUM         ;AL=AX/BYTE_SUM
IDIV WORD_TBL[BX];Indirect address
```

IMUL

Arithmetic

Integer Multiply: If the operand is a byte value, IMUL multiplies AL by the contents of the operand, and stores the result in AX. If the operand is a word value, IMUL multiplies the contents of AX by the contents of the operand, and stores the result in DX:AX. This instruction treats numbers as signed binary values.

Flags affected

OF, CF, SF (undefined), ZF (undefined), AF (undefined), PF (undefined)

Coding examples

```
IMUL  BX             ;DX:AX=AX*BX
IMUL  WRDTMP         ;DX:AX=AX*WRDTMP
IMUL  BYTE_SUM       ;AX=AL*BYTE_SUM
IMUL  WORD_TBL[BX]   ;Indirect address
```

IN

Data-transfer

Input from Port: IN loads a byte or a word from the specified hardware I/O port address to AL or AX, respectively. A port number smaller than 256 may be specified either as a constant or as a variable in the DX register, but a port number greater than 255 *must* be specified in the DX register.

Coding examples

```
IN  AL,64h
IN  AX,DX
```

INC

Arithmetic

Increment: INC changes, by increments of 1, the contents of the operand. The operand is assumed to be an unsigned binary value.

Flags affected
OF, SF, ZF, AF, PF

Coding examples
```
INC AX
INC SUM
INC CL
INC TEMP[SI]
```

INT

Control-transfer

Software Interrupt: INT initiates a software interrupt of the CPU. INT does the following: (1) pushes the flags on the stack; (2) clears the TF and IF flags; (3) pushes the value of CS on the stack; (4) loads CS with the segment address of the interrupt being invoked (found at the calculated address in the interrupt vector table); (5) pushes the value of IP on the stack; and (6) loads IP with the offset address of the interrupt being invoked (found at the calculated address in the interrupt vector table).

Execution then continues at the newly loaded CS:IP address until an IRET instruction is encountered.

Flags affected
IF, TF

Coding examples
```
INT 10h
INT 13h
```

INTO

Control-transfer

Interrupt on Overflow: If the overflow flag (OF) is set, INTO executes an interrupt 4 and control proceeds as though an INT 4 had been issued. Be aware that, in this case, the flags register is affected as described for the INT instruction.

IRET

Control-transfer

Return from Interrupt: IRET causes termination of an interrupt procedure and—by popping the values of IP, CS, and the flags register from the stack—returns control to the point at which the interrupt occurred.

Flags affected
OF, DF, IF, TF, SF, ZF, AF, PF, CF (NT and IOPL for the 80286)

JA

Control-transfer

Jump if Above: JA causes program execution to branch to the operand address if both the carry and zero flags are clear. This instruction is functionally the same as JNBE.

Coding example
```
JA NEXT_STEP
```

JAE

Control-transfer

Jump if Above or Equal: JAE causes program execution to branch to the operand address if the carry flag is clear. This instruction is functionally the same as JNB or JNC.

Coding example
```
JAE NEXT_STEP
```

JB

Control-transfer

Jump if Below: JB causes program execution to branch to the operand address if the carry flag is set. This instruction is functionally the same as JC or JNAE.

Coding example
```
JB NEXT_STEP
```

JBE

Control-transfer

Jump if Below or Equal: JBE causes program execution to branch to the operand address if either the carry or zero flag is set. This instruction is functionally the same as JNA.

Coding example
```
JBE NEXT_STEP
```

JC

Control-transfer

Jump on Carry: JC causes program execution to branch
to the operand address if the carry flag is set. This
instruction is functionally the same as JB or JNAE.

Coding example

```
JC NEXT_STEP
```

JCXZ

Control-transfer

Jump if CX=0: JCXZ causes program execution to
branch to the operand address if the value of CX is 0.

Coding example

```
JCXZ SKIP_LOOP
```

JE

Control-transfer

Jump if Equal: JE causes program execution to branch
to the operand address if the zero flag is set. This
instruction is functionally the same as JZ.

Coding example

```
JE NEXT_STEP
```

JG

Control-transfer

Jump if Greater: JG causes program execution to
branch to the operand address if the sign flag equals the
overflow flag or if the zero flag is clear. This instruction is functionally the same as JNLE.

Coding example
```
JG NEXT_STEP
```

JGE

Control-transfer

Jump if Greater or Equal: JGE causes program execution to branch to the operand address if the sign flag equals the overflow flag. This instruction is functionally the same as JNL.

Coding example
```
JGE NEXT_STEP
```

JL

Control-transfer

Jump if Less Than: JL causes program execution to branch to the operand address if the sign flag does not equal the overflow flag. This instruction is functionally the same as JNGE.

Coding example
```
JL NEXT_STEP
```

JLE

Control-transfer

Jump if Less Than or Equal: JLE causes program execution to branch to the operand address if the sign flag does not equal the overflow flag or if the zero flag is set. This instruction is functionally the same as JNG.

Coding example
```
JLE NEXT_STEP
```

JMP

Control-transfer

Jump: JMP causes program execution to begin execution at the designated operand address. JMP affects the CS and IP registers as necessary to cause this unconditional branch.

Coding examples
```
JMP EXIT_CODE
JMP [BX]          ;Address at [BX]
JMP AX            ;Address in AX
```

JNA

Control-transfer

Jump if Not Above: JNA causes program execution to branch to the operand address if either the carry flag or zero flag is set. This instruction is functionally the same as JBE.

Coding example
```
JNA NEXT_STEP
```

JNAE

Control-transfer

Jump if Not Above or Equal: JNAE causes program execution to branch to the operand address if the carry flag is set. This instruction is functionally the same as JB or JC.

Coding example
```
JNAE NEXT_STEP
```

JNB

Control-transfer

Jump if Not Below: JNB causes program execution to branch to the operand address if the carry flag is clear. This instruction is functionally the same as JAE or JNC.

Coding example

```
JNB NEXT_STEP
```

JNBE

Control-transfer

Jump if Not Below or Equal: JNBE causes program execution to branch to the operand address if both the carry and zero flags are clear. This instruction is functionally the same as JA.

Coding example

```
JNBE NEXT_STEP
```

JNC

Control-transfer

Jump on No Carry: JNC causes program execution to branch to the operand address if the carry flag is clear. This instruction is functionally the same as JAE or JNB.

Coding example

```
JNC NEXT_STEP
```

JNE

Control-transfer

Jump if Not Equal: JNE causes program execution to branch to the operand address if the zero flag is clear. This instruction is functionally the same as JNZ.

Coding example
```
JNE NEXT_STEP
```

JNG

Control-transfer

Jump if Not Greater Than: JNG causes program execution to branch to the operand address if the sign flag does not equal the overflow flag or if the zero flag is set. This instruction is functionally the same as JLE.

Coding example
```
JNG NEXT_STEP
```

JNGE

Control-transfer

Jump if Not Greater Than or Equal: JNGE causes program execution to branch to the operand address if the sign flag does not equal the overflow flag. This instruction is functionally the same as JL.

Coding example
```
JNGE NEXT_STEP
```

JNL

Control-transfer

Jump if Not Less Than: JNL causes program execution to branch to the operand address if the sign flag equals the overflow flag. This instruction is functionally the same as JGE.

Coding example

```
JNL NEXT_STEP
```

JNLE

Control-transfer

Jump if Not Less Than or Equal: JNLE causes program execution to branch to the operand address if the sign flag equals the overflow flag or the zero flag is clear. This instruction is functionally the same as JG.

Coding example

```
JNLE NEXT_STEP
```

JNO

Control-transfer

Jump on No Overflow: JNO causes program execution to branch to the operand address if the overflow flag is clear.

Coding example

```
JNO NEXT_STEP
```

JNP

Control-transfer

Jump on No Parity: JNP causes program execution to branch to the operand address if the parity flag is clear. This instruction is functionally the same as JPO.

Coding example
```
JNP NEXT_STEP
```

JNS

Control-transfer

Jump on Not Sign: JNS causes program execution to branch to the operand address if the sign flag is clear.

Coding example
```
JNS NEXT_STEP
```

JNZ

Control-transfer

Jump on Not Zero: JNZ causes program execution to branch to the operand address if the zero flag is clear. This instruction is functionally the same as JNE.

Coding example
```
JNZ NEXT_STEP
```

JO

Control-transfer

Jump on Overflow: JO causes program execution to branch to the operand address if the overflow flag is set.

Coding example
```
JO NEXT_STEP
```

JP

Control-transfer

Jump on Parity: JP causes program execution to branch to the operand address if the parity flag is set. This instruction is functionally the same as JPE.

Coding example
```
JP NEXT_STEP
```

JPE

Control-transfer

Jump on Parity Even: JPE causes program execution to branch to the operand address if the parity flag is set. This instruction is functionally the same as JP.

Coding example
```
JPE NEXT_STEP
```

JPO

Control-transfer

Jump on Parity Odd: JPO causes program execution to branch to the operand address if the parity flag is clear. This instruction is functionally the same as JNP.

Coding example
```
JPO NEXT_STEP
```

JS

Control-transfer

Jump on Sign: JS causes program execution to branch
to the operand address if the sign flag is set.

Coding example
    JS NEXT_STEP

JZ

Control-transfer

Jump on Zero: JZ causes program execution to branch
to the operand address if the zero flag is set. This
instruction is functionally the same as JE.

Coding example
    JZ NEXT_STEP

LAHF

Data-transfer

Load AH Register with Flags: LAHF copies the low-
order byte of the flags register to AH. After execution
of this instruction, bits 7, 6, 4, 2, and 1 of AH are equal
to SF, ZF, AF, PF, and CF, respectively.

LDS

Data-transfer

Load DS Register: LDS performs two distinct operations: it loads DS with the segment address of the
source operand, and loads the destination operand with
the offset address of the source operand.

Coding example
```
LDS SI,SOURCE_BUFFER
```

LEA

Data-transfer

Load Effective Address: LEA transfers the offset address of the source operand to the destination operand. The destination operand must be a general word register.

Coding example
```
LEA AX,MESSAGE_1
```

LES

Data-transfer

Load ES Register: LES performs two distinct operations: it loads ES with the segment address of the source operand, and loads the destination operand with the offset address of the source operand.

Coding example
```
LES DI,DEST_BUFFER
```

LOCK

Flag- and processor-control

Lock Bus: LOCK prohibits interference from any other coprocessors during the execution of the next instruction issued. LOCK is a prefix to be used with other operations.

Coding example
```
LOCK XLAT
```

#

String-manipulation

Load a Byte from String into AL: This instruction loads AL with the contents of the address pointed to by SI. SI then changes in increments or decrements of 1, depending on the setting of the direction flag. Intel lists this command as LODS; however, various assemblers may distinguish between byte (LODSB) and word (LODSW).

#

String-manipulation

Load a Word from String into AX: This instruction loads AX with the contents of the address pointed to by SI. SI then changes in increments or decrements of 2, depending on the setting of the direction flag. Intel lists this command as LODS; however, various assemblers may distinguish between byte (LODSB) and word (LODSW).

LOOP

Control-transfer

Loop: Based on the contents of CX, program execution branches to the address of the destination operand. If CX does not equal 0, CX changes in decrements of 1,

and the branch occurs. If CX is 0, no decrements or
branching occur, and execution proceeds to the next
instruction.

Coding example
```
LOOP PRINT_LOOP
```

LOOPE
Control-transfer

Loop While Equal: Based on the contents of CX and
the zero flag, program execution branches to the
address of the destination operand. If CX does not
equal 0 and the zero flag is set, CX changes in decrements of 1, and the branch occurs. If CX is 0 or the
zero flag is clear, no decrements or branching occur,
and execution proceeds to the next instruction. This
instruction is functionally equivalent to LOOPZ.

Coding example
```
LOOPE TEST_LOOP
```

LOOPNE
Control-transfer

Loop While Not Equal: Based on the contents of CX
and the zero flag, program execution branches to the
address of the destination operand. If CX does not
equal 0 and the zero flag is clear, CX changes in
decrements of 1, and the branch occurs. If CX is 0 or
the zero flag is set, no decrements or branching occur,
and execution proceeds to the next instruction. This
instruction is functionally equivalent to LOOPNZ.

Coding example
```
LOOPNE TEST_LOOP
```

⹀ LOOPNZ

Control-transfer

Loop While Not Zero: Based on the contents of CX and the zero flag, program execution branches to the address of the destination operand. If CX does not equal 0 and the zero flag is clear, CX changes in decrements of 1, and the branch occurs. If CX is 0 or the zero flag is set, no decrements or branching occur, and execution proceeds to the next instruction. This instruction is functionally equivalent to **LOOPNE**.

Coding example
```
LOOPNZ TEST_LOOP
```

⹀ LOOPZ

Control-transfer

Loop While Zero: Based on the contents of CX and the zero flag, program execution branches to the address of the destination operand. If CX does not equal 0 and the zero flag is set, CX changes in decrements of 1, and the branch occurs. If CX is 0 or the zero flag is clear, no decrements or branching occur, and execution proceeds to the next instruction. This instruction is functionally equivalent to **LOOPE**.

Coding example
```
LOOPZ TEST_LOOP
```

MOV

Data-transfer

Move: MOV copies the contents of the source operand to the destination operand. Both operands must be the same length.

Coding examples

```
MOV  AX,BX           ;AX=BX
MOV  AX,WRDTMP       ;AX=WRDTMP
MOV  WRDSUM,BX       ;WRDSUM=BX
MOV  CL,57           ;CL=57
MOV  DEC,10          ;DEC=10
MOV  AX,TEMP[BX]     ;Indirect address
```

MOVSB

String-manipulation

Move String, Byte-by-Byte: MOVSB moves strings, byte-by-byte. The values of SI and DI change in increments or decrements of 1, depending on the setting of the direction flag. Usually, this instruction is used with the REP instruction to repeat the move for a maximum of CX bytes. Intel lists this command as MOVS; however, various assemblers make the byte/word distinctions.

Coding examples

```
MOVSB
REP MOVSB            ;Repeat a move loop
```

MOVSW

String-manipulation

Move String, Word-by-Word: MOVSW moves strings, word-by-word. The values of SI and DI change in increments or decrements of 2, depending on the setting of the direction flag. Usually, this instruction is

used with the REP instruction to repeat the move for a
maximum of CX words. Intel lists this command as
MOVS; however, various assemblers make the byte/
word distinctions.

Coding examples

```
MOVSW
REP MOVSW                ;Repeat a move loop
```

MUL
Arithmetic

Multiply: If the operand is a byte value, MUL multiplies the contents of AL by the contents of the operand
and stores the result in AX. If the operand is a word
value, MUL multiplies the contents of AX by the
contents of the operand and stores the result in DX:AX.
This instruction treats numbers as unsigned binary
values.

Flags affected

OF, CF, SF (undefined), ZF (undefined), AF (undefined), PF (undefined)

Coding examples

```
MUL BX               ;DX:AX=AX*BX
MUL WORD_TEMP        ;DX:AX=AX*WORD_TEMP
MUL BYTE_SUM         ;AX=AL*BYTE_SUM
MUL WORD_TBL[BX]     ;Indirect address
```

NEG
Arithmetic

Negate: NEG calculates the two's complement of the
destination operand and stores the result in the destination operand. This calculation is effectively the same as
subtracting the destination operand from 0.

Flags affected
> OF, SF, ZF, AF, PF, CF

Coding examples
> ```
> NEG TEMP
> NEG CL
> ```

NOP

Flag- and processor-control

No Operation: NOP simply takes space and time. It causes the CPU to do nothing.

NOT

Bit-manipulation

Logical NOT on Bits: NOT inverts the bits in the destination operand (0 becomes 1, and 1 becomes 0) and stores the inverted bits in the destination operand.

Coding examples
> ```
> NOT CL
> NOT TEMP
> NOT AX
> ```

OR

Bit-manipulation

Logical OR on Bits: This instruction performs a logical OR of the operands and stores the result in the destination operand. Each bit of the resultant byte or word is set to 1 if either or both of the corresponding bits of each operand are set to 1.

Flags affected

OF, SF, ZF, PF, CF, AF (undefined)

Coding examples

```
OR AL, BL
OR AL, 10000000b
OR DX, TEMP
OR AX, CX
```

Data-transfer

Output to Port: OUT sends a byte (AL) or word (AX) to the specified hardware I/O port address. A port number less than 256 may be specified either as a constant or as a variable in the DX register. A port number greater than 255, however, *must* be specified in the DX register.

Coding examples

```
OUT AL, 64h
OUT AX, DX
```

Data-transfer

Remove Data from Stack: POP removes a word from the stack and places that word in the desired destination operand.

Coding examples

```
POP AX
POP DS
POP HOLD_REG
```

POPF
Data-transfer

Remove Flags from Stack: POPF removes a word from the stack and places the word in the flags register.

Flags affected
OF, DF, IF, TF, SF, ZF, AF, PF, CF (NT and IOPL for the 80286)

PUSH
Data-transfer

Place Data on Stack: PUSH places a copy of the value of the operand on the stack.

Coding examples
```
PUSH AX
PUSH DS
PUSH HOLD_REG
```

PUSHF
Data-transfer

Place Flags on Stack: PUSHF places a copy of the flags register on the stack.

RCL
Bit-manipulation

Rotate Left through Carry: RCL rotates all bits in the destination operand to the left by the number of places specified in the source operand. The rotation is performed through the carry flag in an order that rotates the most significant bit of the destination operand to the carry flag, and the carry flag to the least significant bit of the destination operand.

Flags affected
OF, CF

Coding examples
```
RCL AX, 1
RCL BL, 3
RCL TEMP, CL
```

Bit-manipulation

Rotate Right through Carry: RCR rotates all bits in the destination operand to the right by the number of places specified in the source operand. The rotation is performed through the carry flag in an order that rotates the least significant bit of the destination operand to the carry flag, and the carry flag to the most significant bit of the destination operand.

Flags affected
OF, CF

Coding examples
```
RCR AX, 1
RCR BL, 3
RCR TEMP, CL
```

REP

String-manipulation

Repeat: REP causes string-manipulation instructions to be repeated the number of iterations specified in CX.

Coding example
```
REP MOVSB
```

REPE

String-manipulation

Repeat if Equal: REPE causes string-manipulation instructions to be repeated the number of iterations specified in CX. When used with CMPSB, CMPSW, SCASB, or SCASW, this instruction repeats only while the zero flag is set. This instruction is functionally equivalent to REPZ.

Coding example
```
REPE CMPSW
```

REPNE

String-manipulation

Repeat if Not Equal: REPNE causes string-manipulation instructions to be repeated the number of iterations specified in CX. When used with CMPSB, CMPSW, SCASB, or SCASW, this instruction repeats only while the zero flag is clear. This instruction is functionally equivalent to REPNZ.

Coding example
```
REPNE CMPSW
```

REPNZ

String-manipulation

Repeat if Not Zero: REPNZ causes string-manipulation instructions to be repeated the number of iterations specified in CX. When used with CMPSB, CMPSW, SCASB, or SCASW, this instruction repeats only while the zero flag is clear. This instruction is functionally equivalent to REPNE.

Coding example
```
REPNZ CMPSW
```

REPZ

String-manipulation

Repeat if Zero: REPZ causes string-manipulation instructions to be repeated the number of iterations specified in CX. When used with CMPSB, CMPSW, SCASB, or SCASW, this instruction repeats only while the zero flag is set. This instruction is functionally equivalent to REPE.

Coding example
```
REPZ CMPSW
```

RET

Control-transfer

Return from Subroutine: By popping IP from the stack, RET transfers program control back to the point where a CALL was issued. If the CALL was to a FAR procedure, both CS and IP are popped from the stack.

If the RET has a specified return value (2, in the coding example), the stack is adjusted by that number of bytes. The coding example shows that a word is discarded from the stack after either IP or CS:IP is popped.

Coding examples

```
RET
RET 2
```

ROL

Bit-manipulation

Rotate Left: ROL rotates all bits in the destination operand to the left by the number of places specified in the source operand.

Flags affected
OF, CF

Coding examples

```
ROL AX,1
ROL BL,3
ROL TEMP,CL
```

ROR

Bit-manipulation

Rotate Right: ROR rotates all bits in the destination operand to the right by the number of places specified in the source operand.

Flags affected
OF, CF

Coding examples
```
ROR AX,1
ROR BL,3
ROR TEMP,CL
```

SAHF
Data-transfer

Store AH into Flag Register: SAHF copies the contents of AH to the low-order byte of the flags register. After execution of this instruction, SF, ZF, AF, PF, and CF are equal to bits 7, 6, 4, 2, and 1 of AH, respectively.

Flags affected
SF, ZF, AF, PF, CF

SAL
Bit-manipulation

Arithmetic Shift Left: SAL shifts all bits in the destination operand to the left by the number of places specified in the source operand. High-order bits are lost, and low-order bits are cleared.

Flags affected
OF, SF, ZF, PF, CF, AF (undefined)

Coding examples
```
SAL AX,1
SAL BL,3
SAL TEMP,CL
```

SAR

Bit-manipulation

Arithmetic Shift Right: SAR shifts all bits in the destination operand to the right by the number of places specified in the source operand. Low-order bits are lost, and high-order bits are set equal to the existing high-order bit.

Flags affected

OF, SF, ZF, PF, CF, AF (undefined)

Coding examples

```
SAR AX,1
SAR BL,3
SAR TEMP,CL
```

SBB

Arithmetic

Subtract with Carry: SBB subtracts the contents of the source operand from (and stores the result in) the destination operand. If the carry flag is set, the result changes in decrements of 1. In this instruction, the values being added are assumed to be binary.

Flags affected

OF, SF, ZF, AF, PF, CF

Coding examples

```
SBB AX,BX          ;AX=AX-AX-CF
SBB AX,TEMP        ;AX=AX-TEMP-CF
SBB SUM,BX         ;SUM=SUM-BX-CF
SBB CL,10          ;CL=CL-10-CF
SBB AX,TEMP[BX]    ;Indirect address
```

SCASB

String-manipulation

Scan String for Byte: SCASB subtracts the destination operand string byte (pointed to by DI) from the value of AL. The result is not stored, but the flags are updated. Then the value of DI changes in increments or decrements of 1, depending on the setting of the direction flag. Usually, this instruction is used with the REPE, REPNE, REPNZ, or REPZ instructions to repeat the scan for a maximum of CX bytes, or until SCASB finds a match or difference. Intel lists this command as SCAS; however, various assemblers make the byte/word distinctions.

Flags affected
OF, SF, ZF, AF, PF, CF

Coding examples
```
SCASB
REPNZ SCASB          ;Repeat a scan loop
```

SCASW

String-manipulation

Scan String for Word: SCASW subtracts the destination operand string word (pointed to by DI) from the value of AX. The result is not stored, but the flags are updated. Then the value of DI changes in increments or decrements of 2, depending on the setting of the direction flag. Usually, this instruction is used with the REPE, REPNE, REPNZ, or REPZ instructions to repeat the scan for a maximum of CX bytes, or until SCASW finds a match or difference. Intel lists this command as SCAS; however, various assemblers make the byte/word distinctions.

Flags affected

    OF, SF, ZF, AF, PF, CF

Coding examples

```
SCASW
REPNZ SCASW        ;Repeat a scan loop
```

SHL

Bit-manipulation

Shift Left: SHL shifts all bits in the destination operand to the left by the number of places specified in the source operand. High-order bits are lost, and low-order bits are cleared.

Flags affected

    OF, SF, ZF, PF, CF, AF (undefined)

Coding examples

```
SHL AX,1
SHL BL,3
SHL TEMP,CL
```

SHR

Bit-manipulation

Shift Right: SHR shifts all bits in the destination operand to the right by the number of places specified in the source operand. Low-order bits are lost, and high-order bits are cleared.

Flags affected

    OF, SF, ZF, PF, CF, AF (undefined)

Coding examples
```
SHR AX,1
SHR BL,3
SHR TEMP,CL
```

STC
Flag- and processor-control

Set Carry Flag: STC sets the carry flag, regardless of the flag's present condition.

Flags affected
    CF

STD
Flag- and processor-control

Set Direction Flag: STD sets the direction flag, regardless of the flag's present condition. This setting has an effect on the string instructions.

Flags affected
    DF

STI
Flag- and processor-control

Set Interrupt Flag: STI sets the interrupt flag, regardless of the flag's present condition. While this flag is set, the CPU responds to maskable interrupts.

Flags affected
    IF

STOSB

String-manipulation

Store Byte in AL at String: This instruction copies the contents of AL to the byte address pointed to by DI. DI then changes in increments or decrements of 1, depending on the setting of the direction flag. Intel lists this command as STOS; however, various assemblers make the byte/word distinctions.

STOSW

String-manipulation

Store Word in AX at String: This instruction copies the contents of AX to the word address pointed to by DI. DI then changes in increments or decrements of 2, depending on the setting of the direction flag. Intel lists this command as STOS; however, various assemblers make the byte/word distinctions.

SUB

Arithmetic

Subtract: SUB subtracts the contents of the source operand from (and stores the result in) the destination operand. In this instruction, the values being added are assumed to be binary.

Flags affected
OF, SF, ZF, AF, PF, CF

Coding examples
```
SUB AX,BX          ;AX=AX-AX
SUB AX,TEMP        ;AX=AX-TEMP
SUB SUM,BX         ;SUM=SUM-BX
SUB CL,10          ;CL=CL-10
SUB AX,TEMP[BX]    ;Indirect address
```

TEST

Bit-manipulation

Test Bits: TEST performs a logical AND of the operands, but the result is not stored. Only the flags are affected. Each bit of the resultant byte or word is set to 1 only if the corresponding bit of each operand is 1.

Flags affected
OF, SF, ZF, PF, CF, AF (undefined)

Coding examples
```
TEST AX,BX          ;
TEST AX,TEMP        ;TEMP must be a word
TEST SUM,BX         ;SUM must be a word
TEST CL,00001111b;
TEST AX,TEMP[BX]    ;Indirect address
```

WAIT

Flag- and processor-control

Wait: WAIT causes the CPU to wait for an external interrupt on the TEST line before continuing.

XCHG

Data-transfer

Exchange: XCHG swaps the contents of the source and destination operands.

Coding examples
```
XCHG AX,BX          ;Swap AX with BX
XCHG CL,CH          ;Swap CL with CH
XCHG AX,TEMP        ;Swap AX with TEMP
```

XLAT

Data-transfer

Translate: Assuming that the offset address of a 256-byte translation table is contained in BX, this instruction uses the value in AL as a zero-based offset into the table, and subsequently loads AL with the byte value at that calculated offset. This instruction is helpful for translation tables.

XOR

Bit-manipulation

Logical Exclusive-Or on Bits: This instruction performs a logical XOR of the operands and stores the result in the destination operand. Each bit of the resultant byte or word is set to 1 only if the corresponding bit of each operand contains opposite values.

Flags affected
OF, SF, ZF, PF, CF, AF (undefined)

Coding examples
```
XOR AX,BX          ;
XOR AX,TEMP        ;TEMP must be a word
XOR SUM,BX         ;SUM must be a word
XOR CL,0001111b    ;
XOR AX,TEMP[BX]    ;Indirect address
```

Overview of the Intel 80286

The Intel 80286 differs from the 8086/8088, from a programmer's viewpoint, in the instruction set available and the use of flags.

In addition to the standard flags listed for the 8086/8088, the 80286 also contains the following flags:

Abbreviation	Meaning
NT	Nested task
IOPL	I/O privilege level

The instruction set of the 80286 is an extension of the instruction set for the Intel 8086/8088. The 80286 also correctly processes the instructions of the 8086/8088, as detailed earlier in this quick reference. Some of the 27 additional instructions included here are not designed for use in applications software; rather, they are used for developing operating system software.

The following list contains the 27 additional instructions for the Intel 80286. The list is arranged in alphabetical order:

ARPL	LGDT	POPA
BOUND	LIDT	PUSHA
CLTS	LLDT	SGDT
ENTER	LMSW	SIDT
INS	LSL	SLDT
INSB	LTR	SMSW
INSW	OUTS	STR
LAR	OUTSB	VERR
LEAVE	OUTSW	VERW

The following 27 additional instructions for the Intel 80286 are arranged by general instruction classification. Within each classification, instructions are listed in alphabetical order.

Bit-manipulation	LMSW	*Flag- and*
lation	LSL	*processor-*
ARPL	LTR	*control*
	OUTS	BOUND
Data-	OUTSB	CLTS
transfer	OUTSW	ENTER
INS	POPA	LEAVE
INSB	PUSHA	VERR
INSW	SGDT	VERW
LAR	SIDT	
LGDT	SLDT	
LIDT	SMSW	
LLDT	STR	

The following table details how the additional 80286 instructions affect flags. An *X* in a column indicates that the flag is changed by the instruction; a question mark indicates that the flag is undefined after the instruction is executed. Only those instructions that affect flags are included in this table.

Inst.	*OF*	*DF*	*IF*	*TF*	*SF*	*ZF*	*AF*	*PF*	*CF*
ARPL						X			
LAR						X			
LSL						X			
VERR						X			
VERW						X			

Instruction Set for the Intel 80286

The instructions presented in this section function as described on the 80286 and the 80386.

ARPL

Bit-manipulation

Adjust RPL Field of Selector: ARPL compares the RPL bits (bits 0 and 1) of the first operand with those of the second. If the RPL bits of the first operand are less than those of the second, the two bits of the first operand are set equal to the two bits of the second, and the zero flag is set. Otherwise, the zero flag is cleared. This instruction is used only in operating system software (not used in applications software).

Flags affected
  ZF

Coding examples
```
ARPL SELECTOR,AX
ARPL AX,CX
```

BOUND

Flag- and processor-control

Check Array Index against Bounds: BOUND determines whether the signed value in the first operand falls between the two boundaries specified by the second operand. The word at the second operand is assumed to be the lower boundary, and the following word is assumed to be the upper boundary. An interrupt 5 occurs if the value in the first operand is less than the lower limit or greater than the upper limit.

Coding example
```
BOUND BX,LIMITS
```

Flag- and processor-control

Clear Task Switched Flag: CLTS clears the task-switched flag of the machine status register. This instruction is used only in operating system software (not in applications software).

Flags affected
None in flags register—affects machine status word

Flag- and processor-control

Make Stack Frame for Procedure Parameters: ENTER modifies the stack appropriately for entry to a high-level language procedure. The first operand specifies the number of bytes of storage to be allocated on the stack; the second operand specifies the nesting level of the routine. The effects of this instruction are undone by the LEAVE instruction.

Coding examples
```
ENTER PPTR,3
ENTER DS:BX,0
```

Data-transfer

Input String from Port: INS loads a byte or a word from the specified hardware I/O port address to the destination operand. The size of the destination operand determines whether a byte or a word is transferred. The port number may range from 0 to 65,535.

Coding examples

```
INS CX,DX          ;Load word
INS BL,DX          ;Load byte
```

Data-transfer

Input String Byte from Port: INSB loads a byte from the hardware I/O port address specified in DX to the address specified by ES:[DI]. The port number may range from 0 to 65,535. After the transfer, DI changes in an increment or decrement of 1, depending on the setting of the direction flag.

Data-transfer

Input String Word from Port: INSW loads a word from the hardware I/O port address specified in DX to the address specified by ES:[DI]. The port number may range from 0 to 65,535. After the transfer, DI changes in increments or decrements of 2, depending on the setting of the direction flag.

LAR

Data-transfer

Load Access-Rights Byte: Based on the selection in the second operand, the high byte of the destination register is overwritten by the value of the access-rights byte, and the low byte is zeroed. The loading is done only if the descriptor is visible at the current privilege level and at the selector RPL. The zero flag is set if the loading operation is successful.

Flags affected
ZF

Coding example
```
LAR AX,SELECT
```

LEAVE

Flag- and processor-control

High-Level Procedure Exit: LEAVE undoes the changes performed by the ENTER instruction. This instruction is used for exiting high-level language subroutines.

LGDT

Data-transfer

Load Global Descriptor Table Register: LGDT loads the six bytes associated with the global descriptor table from the memory address specified in the operand. This instruction is for use in protected-mode operating system software; it is not used in applications software.

Coding example
```
LGDT TEMP[BX]
```

LIDT

Data-transfer

Load Interrupt Descriptor Table Register: LIDT loads the six bytes associated with the interrupt descriptor table from the memory address specified in the operand. This instruction is for use in protected-mode operating system software; it is not used in applications software.

Coding example
```
LIDT TEMP[BX]
```

LLDT

Data-transfer

Load Local Descriptor Table Register: Based on the selector specified in the operand, LLDT transfers the valid global descriptor table entry to the local descriptor table. This instruction is for use in protected-mode operating system software (not in applications software).

Coding example
```
LLDT AX
```

LMSW

Data-transfer

Load Machine Status Word: LMSW copies the value of the operand to the machine status word. This instruction is for use only in operating system software (not in applications software).

Coding example
```
LMSW AX
```

LSL

Data-transfer

Load Segment Limit: Based on the selector specified in the source operand, LSL loads the descriptor's limit field into the target operand (register). The descriptor denoted by the selector must be visible. If the loading is successful, the zero flag is set; otherwise, it is cleared.

Flags affected
ZF

Coding example
```
LSL AX, SELECTOR
```

LTR

Data-transfer

Load Task Register: LTR loads the task register from the value of the source operand. This instruction is for use in operating system software only and is not used in applications software.

Coding examples
```
LTR DX
LTR TEMP[BX]
```

OUTS

Data-transfer

Output String to Port: OUTS sends a byte or a word (length is specified by the size of the source operand) to the hardware I/O port address specified in DX. The port number may range from 0 to 65,535.

Coding examples

```
OUTS DX,CX      ;Output word
OUTS DX,BL      ;Output byte
```

OUTSB

Data-transfer

Output String Byte to Port: OUTSB sends a byte from the address specified by DS:[SI] to the hardware I/O port address specified in DX. The port number may range from 0 to 65,535. After the transfer, DI changes in an increment or decrement of 1, depending on the setting of the direction flag.

OUTSW

Data-transfer

Output String Word to Port: OUTSW sends a word from the address specified by DS:[SI] to the hardware I/O port address specified in DX. The port number may range from 0 to 65,535. After the transfer, DI changes in increments or decrements of 2, depending on the setting of the direction flag.

POPA

Data-transfer

Pop All General Registers: POPA removes the general-purpose registers and loads them from the stack in this order: DI, SI, BP, SP, BX, DX, CX, AX. The SP register is discarded when it is popped.

PUSHA

Data-transfer

Push All General Registers: The general-purpose registers are pushed on the stack in this order: AX, CX, DX, BX, SP, BP, SI, DI. The SP value that is pushed is the value existing before this instruction is executed.

SGDT

Data-transfer

Store Global Descriptor Table Register: SGDT transfers the six bytes of the global descriptor table to the memory address specified in the operand. This instruction is for use in protected-mode operating system software and is not used in applications software.

Coding example
```
SGDT TEMP[BX]
```

SIDT

Data-transfer

Store Interrupt Descriptor Table Register: SIDT transfers the six bytes of the interrupt descriptor table to the memory address specified in the operand. This instruction is for use in protected-mode operating system software and is not used in applications software.

Coding example
```
SIDT TEMP[BX]
```

SLDT

Data-transfer

Store Local Descriptor Table Register: SLDT copies the contents of the local descriptor table to the two bytes of the operand. This instruction is for use in protected-mode operating system software and is not used in applications software.

Coding examples

```
SLDT AX
SLDT LDT_TEMP
```

SMSW

Data-transfer

Store Machine Status Word: SMSW copies the value of the machine status word to the operand. This instruction is for use in operating system software only and is not used in applications software.

Coding examples

```
SMSW AX
SMSW MSW_TEMP
```

STR

Data-transfer

Store Task Register: STR copies the value of the task register to the operand. This instruction is for use in operating system software only and is not used in applications software.

Coding examples

```
STR AX
STR MSW_TEMP
```

VERR

Flag- and processor-control

Verify a Segment for Reading: VERR determines whether the selector specified in the operand is visible at the current privilege level and is readable. The zero flag is set if the selector is accessible.

Flags affected
ZF

Coding examples
    VERR TEMP
    VERR AX

VERW

Flag- and processor-control

Verify a Segment for Writing: VERW determines whether the selector specified in the operand is visible at the current privilege level and can be written. The zero flag is set if the selector is accessible.

Flags affected
ZF

Coding examples
    VERW TEMP
    VERW AX

Overview of the Intel 80386

Many more differences exist between the 80386 and earlier generations of microprocessors than between the 80286 and the 8086/8088. The differences (from a programmer's viewpoint) have to do with registers, flags, and the instruction set.

80386 Registers

Unlike its 8-bit and 16-bit predecessors, the 80386 is a 32-bit microprocessor. The registers in the 80386 reflect this enlarged structure. The 80386 still uses the same general-purpose registers as the 8086/8088 and the 80286 (AX, BX, CX, and DX), but the registers' full 32-bit counterparts are addressed by use of the E (extended) prefix. EAX, EBX, ECX, and EDX are 32-bit general-purpose registers. Without the E, only the lower 16 bits of each register are accessed. Using the traditional AL, AH, BL, BH, CL, CH, DL, or DH allows access to 8-bit chunks of the lower 16 bits of the registers.

This use of the E prefix to denote 32-bit register size also applies to other microprocessor registers, such as BP, SI, DI, and SP, which become EBP, ESI, EDI, and ESP, respectively.

The other segment registers—CS, DS, SS, and ES—are intact as implemented in earlier Intel microprocessors. These registers still are 16 bits in width. They are joined, however, by two new segment registers (also 16 bits in width): the FS and GS registers, which operate the same as the ES register.

80386 Flags

As in earlier microprocessors, the 80386 uses a flags register, but it is 32 bits wide. The upper 14 bits of this register are reserved, however, and are not available to programmers. The remaining 18 bits are the ones about which programmers must be concerned. The detailed description of each instruction indicates how these 18 flag bits are affected by execution of the instruction.

In addition to the standard flags listed for the 8086/8088, the 80386 also contains the following flags:

Abbreviation	Meaning
VM	Virtual mode
R	Resume
NT	Nested task
IOPL	I/O privilege level

80386 Instruction Set

The Intel 80386 instruction set is an extension of the instruction set for the Intel 80286 and, subsequently, for the Intel 8086/8088. The 80386 instruction set has 57 more instructions than are available for the 80286. Some of these new instructions are used for developing operating system software; none is designed for use in applications software.

This section does not include instructions listed earlier in this quick reference. It includes only the extensions available specifically with the 80386 and those instructions that change operationally when you use the 32-bit registers of the 80386.

The 57 instructions added with the 80386 are shown in the following list:

BSF	LSS	SETC
BSR	MOVSD	SETE
BT	MOVSX	SETG
BTC	MOVZX	SETGE
BTR	OUTSD	SETL
BTS	POPAD	SETLE
CDQ	POPFD	SETNA
CMPSD	PUSHAD	SETNAE
CWDE	PUSHFD	SETNB
INSD	SCASD	SETNBE
JECXZ	SETA	SETNC
LFS	SETAE	SETNE
LGS	SETB	SETNG
LODSD	SETBE	SETNGE

SETNL	SETNZ	SETS
SETNLE	SETO	SETZ
SETNO	SETP	SHLD
SETNP	SETPE	SHRD
SETNS	SETPO	STOSD

The following list shows those instructions changed from their respective implementations in either the 8086/8088 or the 80286:

ADC	MOV	REPNZ
ADD	MUL	REPZ
AND	NEG	ROL
CMP	NOT	ROR
DEC	OR	SAL
DIV	OUT	SAR
IDIV	POP	SBB
IMUL	PUSH	SHL
IN	RCL	SHR
INC	RCR	SUB
INS	REP	TEST
LAR	REPE	XCHG
LEA	REPNE	XOR

The following list contains the 57 additional instructions for the Intel 80386, arranged by general instruction classification. Within each classification, instructions are listed in alphabetical order.

Arithmetic	SHLD	LSS
CDQ	SHRD	MOVSX
CWDE		MOVZX
	Control-	OUTSD
	transfer	POPAD
Bit-manipu-	JECXZ	POPFD
lation		PUSHAD
BSF		PUSHFD
BSR	*Data-*	SETA
BT	*transfer*	SETAE
BTC	INSD	SETB
BTR	LFS	SETBE
BTS	LGS	

SETC	SETNG	SETS
SETE	SETNGE	SETZ
SETG	SETNL	
SETGE	SETNLE	*String-*
SETL	SETNO	*manipula-*
SETLE	SETNP	*tion*
SETNA	SETNS	CMPSD
SETNAE	SETNZ	LODSD
SETNB	SETO	MOVSD
SETNBE	SETP	SCASD
SETNC	SETPE	STOSD
SETNE	SETPO	

The following table shows how the additional 80386 instructions affect flags. An *X* in a column indicates that the flag is changed by the instruction; a question mark indicates that the flag is undefined after the instruction is executed. Only those instructions that affect flags are included in this table.

Inst.	*OF*	*DF*	*IF*	*TF*	*SF*	*ZF*	*AF*	*PF*	*CF*
BSF						X			
BSR						X			
BT									X
BTC									X
BTR									X
BTS									X
CMPSD	X				X	X	X	X	X
LAR						X			
SCASD	X				X	X	X	X	X
SHLD	?				X	X	?	X	X
SHRD	?				X	X	?	X	X

Instruction Set for the Intel 80386

The instructions presented in this section function as described on the 80386.

 ADC

Arithmetic

Add with Carry: ADC adds the contents of the source operand to (and stores the result in) the destination operand. If the carry flag is set, the result changes in an increment of 1. In this routine, the values being added are assumed to be binary.

Flags affected
OF, SF, ZF, AF, PF, CF

Coding examples
```
ADC AX,BX          ;AX=AX+BX+CF
ADC EAX,TEMP       ;EAX=EAX+TEMP+CF
ADC SUM,EBX        ;SUM=SUM+EBX+CF
ADC CL,10          ;CL=CL+10+CF
ADC AX,TEMP[BX]    ;Indirect address
```

 ADD

Arithmetic

Add: ADD adds the contents of the source operand to (and stores the result in) the destination operand. In this routine, the values being added are assumed to be binary.

Flags affected
OF, SF, ZF, AF, PF, CF

Coding examples
```
ADD  AX,BX         ; AX=AX+BX
ADD  EAX,TEMP      ; EAX=EAX+TEMP
ADD  SUM,EBX       ; SUM=SUM+EBX
ADD  CL,10         ; CL=CL+10
ADD  AX,TEMP[BX]   ; Indirect address
```

AND
Bit-manipulation

Logical AND on Bits: This instruction performs a
logical AND of the operands and stores the result in the
destination operand. Each bit of the resultant byte or
word is set to 1, only if the corresponding bit of each
operand also is set to 1. The carry and overflow flags
are cleared by this operation.

Flags affected
OF, SF, ZF, PF, CF, AF (undefined)

Coding examples
```
AND  AX,BX         ;
AND  EAX,TEMP      ; TEMP must be a dword
AND  SUM,EBX       ; SUM must be a dword
AND  CL,00001111b  ; Zero high nibble
AND  AX,TEMP[BX]   ; Indirect address
```

BSF
Bit-manipulation

Bit Scan Forward: BSF scans the bits of the second
operand (starting with bit 0) to see whether any are set.
If all bits are clear (second operand is 0), the first
operand is not changed, and the zero flag is set. If any
bit is set, the zero flag is cleared, and the first operand
is set equal to the bit number of the bit that is set.

Flags affected
ZF

Coding examples
    BSF EAX,TEMP
    BSF CX,BX

BSR

Bit-manipulation

Bit Scan Reverse: BSR scans the bits of the second
operand (starting with the high-order bit) to see
whether any are set. If all bits are clear (second operand
is 0), the first operand is not changed, and the zero flag
is set. If any bit is set, the zero flag is cleared, and the
first operand is set equal to the bit number of the bit
that is set.

Flags affected
ZF

Coding examples
    BSR EAX,TEMP
    BSR CX,BX

BT

Bit-manipulation

Bit Test: BT uses the value of the second operand as a
bit index into the value of the first operand. The bit at
the indexed position of the first operand is copied into
the carry flag.

Flags affected
CF

Coding examples
```
BT  TEMP,EAX
BT  BX,CX
BT  TEMP,3              ;Test third bit
```

BTC

Bit-manipulation

Bit Test and Complement: BTC uses the value of the second operand as a bit index into the value of the first operand. The opposite value of the bit at the indexed position of the first operand is copied into the carry flag.

Flags affected
CF

Coding examples
```
BTC  TEMP,EAX
BTC  BX,CX
BTC  TEMP,3            ;Opposite of 3rd bit
```

BTR

Bit-manipulation

Bit Test and Reset: BTR uses the value of the second operand as a bit index into the value of the first operand. The bit at the indexed position of the first operand is copied into the carry flag, and then the original bit value is cleared.

Flags affected
CF

Coding examples

```
BTR TEMP,EAX
BTR BX,CX
BTR TEMP,3          ;Value of 3rd bit
```

BTS

Bit-manipulation

Bit Test and Set: BTS uses the value of the second operand as a bit index into the value of the first operand. The bit at the indexed position of the first operand is copied into the carry flag, and then the original bit value is set.

Flags affected

CF

Coding examples

```
BTS TEMP,EAX
BTS BX,CX
BTS TEMP,3          ;Value of 3rd bit
```

CDQ

Arithmetic

Convert Doubleword to Quadword: CDQ converts the doubleword value in EAX to a quadword value in EDX:EAX by extending the high-order bit value of EAX through all bits of EDX.

CMP

Arithmetic

Compare: CMP is considered an arithmetic instruction because the source operand is subtracted from the destination operand. The result, however, is used for setting the flags—it is not stored anywhere. Subsequent testing of the flags can be used for program control.

Flags affected
OF, SF, ZF, AF, PF, CF

Coding examples
```
CMP  AX,BX          ;
CMP  AX,TEMP        ;TEMP must be a word
CMP  SUM,EBX        ;SUM must be a dword
CMP  CL,3           ;Compare to constant
CMP  AX,TEMP[BX]    ;Indirect address
```

CMPSD

String-manipulation

Compare Strings, Doubleword-for-Doubleword: This instruction compares strings, doubleword-for-double-word. EDI and ESI change in increments or decrements of 4, depending on the setting of the direction flag. Usually, this instruction is used with REPE, REPNE, REPNZ, or REPZ instructions to repeat the comparison for a maximum of ECX number of words. This instruction affects only the flags; no changes are made to the operands.

Flags affected
OF, SF, ZF, AF, PF, CF

Coding examples
```
CMPSD               ;Compare strings
REPE CMPSD          ;Repeat a loop
```

CWDE

Arithmetic

Convert Word to Doubleword: CWDE converts the word value in AX to a doubleword value in EAX by extending the high-order bit value of AX through the remaining bits of EAX.

DEC

Arithmetic

Decrement: DEC changes the contents of the operand in decrements of 1. The operand is assumed to be an unsigned binary value.

Flags affected
OF, SF, ZF, AF, PF

Coding examples
```
DEC  AX
DEC  ECX
DEC  SUM
DEC  BL
DEC  TEMP[SI]
```

DIV

Arithmetic

Divide: If the operand is a byte value, DIV divides the contents of AX by the contents of the operand and stores the result in AL and the remainder in AH. If the operand is a word value, DIV divides the contents of DX:AX by the contents of the operand and stores the result in AX and the remainder in DX. If the operand is a doubleword value, DIV divides the contents of EDX:EAX by the contents of the operand and stores the result in EAX and the remainder in EDX. This instruction treats numbers as unsigned binary values.

Flags affected
OF (undefined), SF (undefined), ZF (undefined), AF (undefined), PF (undefined), CF (undefined)

Coding examples
```
DIV BX              ;AX=DX:AX/BX
DIV WORD_TEMP       ;AX=DX:AX/WORD_TEMP
DIV BYTE_SUM        ;AL=AX/BYTE_SUM
DIV DWORDSUM        ;EAX=EDX:EAX/DWORDSUM
DIV WORD_TBL[BX]    ;Indirect address
```

IDIV

Arithmetic

Integer Divide: If the operand is a byte value, IDIV divides the contents of AX by the contents of the operand and stores the result in AL and the remainder in AH. If the operand is a word value, IDIV divides the contents of DX:AX by the contents of the operand and stores the result in AX and the remainder in DX. If the operand is a doubleword value, IDIV divides the contents of EDX:EAX by the contents of the operand and stores the result in EAX and the remainder in EDX. This instruction treats numbers as signed binary values.

Flags affected
OF (undefined), SF (undefined), ZF (undefined), AF (undefined), PF (undefined), CF (undefined)

Coding examples
```
IDIV BX             ;AX=DX:AX/BX
IDIV WORD_TEMP      ;AX=DX:AX/WORD_TEMP
IDIV BYTE_SUM       ;AL=AX/BYTE_SUM
IDIV DWD_SUM        ;EAX=EDX:EAX/DWD_SUM
IDIV WORD_TBL[BX]   ;Indirect address
```

IMUL

Arithmetic

Integer Multiply: The results of this operation depend on the number of operands specified.

If only one operand is given, it is multiplied by either AL, AX, or EAX. If the operand is a byte value, IMUL multiplies the contents of AL by the contents of the operand and stores the result in AX. If the operand is a word value, IMUL multiplies the contents of AX by the contents of the operand and stores the result in DX:AX.

If two operands are given, IMUL multiplies the first operand by the second one and stores the result in the first operand. Both operands must agree in size.

If three operands are given and the third operand is an immediate value, IMUL multiplies the second operand by the third one and stores the result in the first operand.

This instruction treats numbers as signed binary values.

Flags affected

OF, CF, SF (undefined), ZF (undefined), AF (undefined), PF (undefined)

Coding examples

```
IMUL BX              ;DX:AX=AX*BX
IMUL WORD_TEMP       ;DX:AX=AX*WORD_TEMP
IMUL BYTE_SUM        ;AX=AL*BYTE_SUM
IMUL WORD_TBL[BX]    ;Indirect address
IMUL ECX,DWRD,10     ;ECX=DWRD*10
```

IN

Data-transfer

Input from Port: IN loads a byte, word, or doubleword to AL, AX, or EAX, respectively, from the specified hardware I/O port address. A port number less than 256

may be specified as a constant or as a variable in the
DX register. A port number greater than 255, however,
must be specified in the DX register.

Coding examples
```
IN  AL,64h
IN  AX,DX
IN  EAX,DX
```

INC
Arithmetic

Increment: INC changes the contents of the operand in
increments of 1. The operand is assumed to be an
unsigned binary value.

Flags affected
OF, SF, ZF, AF, PF

Coding examples
```
INC AX
INC SUM
INC CL
INC EDI
INC TEMP[SI]
```

INS
Data-transfer

Input String from Port: INS loads a byte, word, or
doubleword from the specified hardware I/O port
address (indicated by the value in DX) to the destination operand. The size of the destination operand
determines whether a byte, word, or doubleword is
transferred. If the destination operand is an offset
address, that address is relative to the ES register. No
segment override is possible.

Coding examples
```
INS CX,DX          ;Load word
INS BL,DX          ;Load byte
INS EAX,DX         ;Load doubleword
```

INSD

Data-transfer

Input String Doubleword from Port: INSD loads a word from the hardware I/O port address specified in DX to the address specified by ES:[EDI]. After the transfer, EDI changes in increments or decrements of 4, depending on the setting of the direction flag.

JECXZ

Control-transfer

Jump if ECX=0: JECXZ causes program execution to branch to the operand address if the value of ECX is zero.

Coding example
```
JECXZ SKIP_LOOP
```

LAR

Data-transfer

Load Access-Rights Byte: Based on the selection in the second operand, the high byte of the destination register is overwritten by the value of the access-rights byte, and the low byte is zeroed. The loading is done only if the descriptor is visible at the current privilege level and at the selector RPL. The zero flag is set if the loading operation is successful.

Flags affected
    ZF

Coding example
    LAR AX,SELECT

LEA

Data-transfer

Load Effective Address: LEA transfers the offset
address of the source operand to the destination
operand. The destination operand must be a general
word or doubleword register.

Coding examples
    LEA AX,MESSAGE_1
    LEA EBX,SOURCE_BLOCK

LFS

Data-transfer

Load FS Register: LFS performs two distinct operations: it loads FS with the segment address of the
source operand, and then loads the destination operand
with the offset address of the source operand.

Coding example
    LFS DI,DEST_BUFFER

LGS

Data-transfer

Load GS Register: LGS performs two distinct operations: it loads GS with the segment address of the
source operand, and then loads the destination operand
with the offset address of the source operand.

Coding example
```
LGS DI,DEST_BUFFER
```

LODSD

String-manipulation

Load a Doubleword from String into EAX: LODSD
loads EAX with the contents of the address pointed to
by ESI. ESI then changes in increments or decrements
of 4, depending on the setting of the direction flag.

LSS

Data-transfer

Load SS Register: LSS performs two distinct operations: it loads SS with the segment address of the
source operand, and then loads the destination operand
with the offset address of the source operand.

Coding example
```
LSS DI,DEST_BUFFER
```

MOV

Data-transfer

Move: MOV copies the contents of the source operand
to the destination operand. When the source operand is
not an immediate value, both operands must agree in
length. If the source or destination operand is a doubleword register, the other register can be a special
register, such as CR0, CR2, CR3, DR0, DR1, DR2,
DR3, DR6, DR7, TR6, or TR7.

Coding examples

```
MOV AX,BX           ;AX=BX
MOV EAX,TEMP        ;EAX=TEMP
MOV SUM,BX          ;SUM=BX
MOV CL,57           ;CL=57
MOV DECIMAL,10      ;DECIMAL=10
MOV AX,TEMP[BX]     ;Indirect address
```

MOVSD
String-manipulation

Move String, Doubleword-by-Doubleword: MOVSD moves strings, doubleword-by-doubleword. The values of ESI and EDI change in increments or decrements of 4, depending on the setting of the direction flag. Usually, this instruction is used with the REP instruction to repeat the move for a maximum of ECX words.

Coding examples

```
MOVSD
REP MOVSD          ;Repeat a move loop
```

MOVSX
Data-transfer

Move with Sign Extended: MOVSX moves the source operand to the destination operand and extends the high-order bit to the balance of the bits in the destination operand. The source operand must be smaller than the destination operand.

Coding examples

```
MOVSX EAX,BX        ;EAX=BX
MOVSX EAX,TEMP      ;EAX=TEMP
MOVSX CX,AL         ;CX=AL
```

MOVZX

Data-transfer

Move with Zero Extended: MOVZX moves the source operand to the destination operand and clears the remaining bits in the destination operand. The source operand must be smaller than the destination operand.

Coding examples
```
MOVZX EAX,BX      ; EAX=BX
MOVZX EAX,TEMP    ; EAX=TEMP
MOVZX CX,AL       ; CX=AL
```

MUL

Arithmetic

Multiply: If the operand is a byte value, MUL multiplies the contents of AL by the contents of the operand and stores the result in AX. If the operand is a word value, MUL multiplies the contents of AX by the contents of the operand and stores the result in DX:AX. If the operand is a doubleword value, MUL multiplies the contents of EAX by the contents of the operand and stores the result in EDX:EAX. This instruction treats numbers as unsigned binary values.

Flags affected
OF, CF, SF (undefined), ZF (undefined), AF (undefined), PF (undefined)

Coding examples
```
MUL BX              ; DX:AX=AX*BX
MUL ECX             ; EDX:EAX=EAX*ECX
MUL WORD_TEMP       ; DX:AX=AX*WORD_TEMP
MUL BYTE_SUM        ; AX=AL*BYTE_SUM
MUL WORD_TBL[BX]    ; Indirect address
```

NEG

Arithmetic

Negate: NEG calculates the two's complement of the destination operand and stores the result in the destination operand. This calculation is effectively the same as subtracting the destination operand from 0.

Flags affected
OF, SF, ZF, AF, PF, CF

Coding examples
```
NEG  TEMP
NEG  CL
NEG  EAX
```

NOT

Bit-manipulation

Logical NOT on Bits: NOT inverts the bits that make up the destination operand (0 becomes 1, and 1 becomes 0) and stores them in the destination operand.

Coding examples
```
NOT  CL
NOT  BYTE_SUM       ;Use byte value
NOT  WORD_SUM       ;Use word value
NOT  DWORD_SUM      ;Use doubleword value
NOT  AX
NOT  EBX
```

OR

Bit-manipulation

Logical OR on Bits: OR performs a logical OR of the operands and stores the result in the destination operand. Each bit of the resultant byte or word is set to 1 if either or both of the corresponding bits of each operand are set to 1.

Flags affected
OF, SF, ZF, PF, CF, AF (undefined)

Coding examples
```
OR  AL,BL
OR  EAX,0FFFFh
OR  DX,TEMP
OR  AX,CX
```

OUT

Data-transfer

Output to Port: OUT sends a byte (AL), word (AX), or doubleword (EAX) to the specified hardware I/O port address. A port number less than 256 may be specified as a constant or as a variable in the DX register. A port number greater than 255, however, *must* be specified in the DX register.

Coding examples
```
OUT 64h,AL
OUT DX,AX
OUT DX,EAX
```

OUTSD

Data-transfer

Output String Doubleword to Port: OUTSD sends a word from the address specified by DS:[ESI] to the hardware I/O port address specified in DX. After the transfer, DI changes in increments or decrements of 4, depending on the setting of the direction flag.

POP

Data-transfer

Remove Data from Stack: POP removes a word or a doubleword (depending on the size of the operand) from the stack and places that word or doubleword in the desired destination operand.

Coding examples
```
POP AX
POP DS
POP GS
POP HOLD_REG
```

POPAD

Data-transfer

Pop All General Doubleword Registers: POPAD removes and loads the general-purpose registers from the stack in this order: EDI, ESI, EBP, ESP, EBX, EDX, ECX, EAX. The ESP register is discarded when it is popped.

POPFD

Data-transfer

Remove Extended Flags from Stack: POPFD removes a doubleword from the stack and places that doubleword in the extended flags register.

Flags affected:
VM, R, NT, IOPL, OF, DF, IF, TF, SF, ZF, AF, PF, CF

PUSH

Data-transfer

Place Data on Stack: PUSH places a copy of the value of the operand on the stack.

Coding examples
```
PUSH AX
PUSH EBX
PUSH DS
PUSH HOLD_REG
```

PUSHAD

Data-transfer

Push All General Doubleword Registers: PUSHAD pushes the general-purpose doubleword registers on the stack in this order: EAX, ECX, EDX, EBX, ESP, EBP, ESI, EDI. The ESP value pushed is the value existing before this instruction is executed.

PUSHFD

Data-transfer

Place Extended Flags on Stack: PUSHFD places a copy of the extended flags register on the stack.

RCL

Bit-manipulation

Rotate Left through Carry: RCL rotates all bits in the destination operand to the left by the number of places specified in the source operand. The rotation is done through the carry flag in an order that rotates the most significant bit of the destination operand to the carry flag, and the carry flag to the least significant bit of the destination operand.

Flags affected
OF, CF

Coding examples
```
RCL AX,1
RCL BL,3
RCL EDX,16
RCL TEMP,CL
```

RCR

Bit-manipulation

Rotate Right through Carry: RCR rotates all bits in the destination operand to the right by the number of places specified in the source operand. The rotation is done through the carry flag in an order that rotates the least significant bit of the destination operand to the carry flag, and the carry flag to the most significant bit of the destination operand.

Flags affected
OF, CF

Coding examples
```
RCR AX,1
RCR BL,3
RCR EDX,16
RCR TEMP,CL
```

REP

String-manipulation

Repeat: REP causes string-manipulation instructions to be repeated the number of iterations specified in CX (if this instruction is used with byte or word operands) or ECX (if this instruction is used with doubleword operands).

Coding example

```
REP MOVSB
```

REPE

String-manipulation

Repeat if Equal: REPE causes string-manipulation instructions to be repeated the number of iterations specified in CX (if this instruction is used with byte or word operands) or ECX (if this instruction is used with doubleword operands). When used with CMPSB, CMPSW, SCASB, or SCASW, this instruction repeats only while the zero flag is set. This instruction is functionally equivalent to REPZ.

Coding example

```
REPE CMPSW
```

REPNE

String-manipulation

Repeat if Not Equal: REPNE causes string-manipula-tion instructions to be repeated the number of iterations specified in CX (if this instruction is used with byte or word operands) or ECX (if this instruction is used with

doubleword operands). When used with CMPSB,
CMPSW, SCASB, or SCASW, REPNE repeats only
while the zero flag is clear. This instruction is functionally equivalent to REPNZ.

Coding example
```
REPNE CMPSW
```

String-manipulation

Repeat if Not Zero: REPNZ causes string-manipulation
instructions to be repeated the number of iterations
specified in CX (if this instruction is used with byte or
word operands) or ECX (if this instruction is used with
doubleword operands). When used with CMPSB,
CMPSW, SCASB, or SCASW, this instruction repeats
only while the zero flag is clear. This instruction is
functionally equivalent to REPNE.

Coding example
```
REPNZ CMPSW
```

String-manipulation

Repeat if Zero: REPZ causes string-manipulation
instructions to be repeated the number of iterations
specified in CX (if this instruction is used with byte or
word operands) or ECX (if this instruction is used with
doubleword operands). When used with CMPSB,
CMPSW, SCASB, or SCASW, this instruction repeats
only while the zero flag is set. This instruction is
functionally equivalent to REPE.

Coding example
```
REPZ CMPSW
```

ROL

Bit-manipulation

Rotate Left: ROL rotates all bits in the destination operand to the left by the number of places specified in the source operand.

Flags affected
OF, CF

Coding examples
```
ROL EAX,1
ROL BL,3
ROL DX,16
ROL TEMP,CL
```

ROR

Bit-manipulation

Rotate Right: ROR rotates all bits in the destination operand to the right by the number of places specified in the source operand.

Flags affected
OF, CF

Coding examples
```
ROR EAX,1
ROR BL,3
ROR DX,16
ROR TEMP,CL
```

SAL

Bit-manipulation

Arithmetic Shift Left: SAL shifts all bits in the destination operand to the left by the number of places specified in the source operand. High-order bits are lost, and low-order bits are cleared.

Flags affected
OF, SF, ZF, PF, CF, AF (undefined)

Coding examples
```
SAL EAX,1
SAL BL,3
SAL DX,16
SAL TEMP,CL
```

SAR

Bit-manipulation

Arithmetic Shift Right: SAR shifts all bits in the destination operand to the right by the number of places specified in the source operand. Low-order bits are lost, and high-order bits are set equal to the existing high-order bit.

Flags affected
OF, SF, ZF, PF, CF, AF (undefined)

Coding examples
```
SAR EAX,1
SAR BL,3
SAR DX,16
SAR TEMP,CL
```

SBB

Arithmetic

Subtract with Carry: SBB subtracts the contents of the source operand from (and stores the result in) the destination operand. If the carry flag is set, the result changes in a decrement of 1. In this instruction, the values being added are assumed to be binary.

Flags affected
OF, SF, ZF, AF, PF, CF

Coding examples
```
SBB AX,BX          ;AX=AX-AX-CF
SBB AX,TEMP        ;AX=AX-TEMP-CF
SBB SUM,EBX        ;SUM=SUM-EBX-CF
SBB CL,10          ;CL=CL-10-CF
SBB AX,TEMP[BX]    ;Indirect address
```

SCASD

String-manipulation

Scan String for Doubleword: SCASD subtracts the destination operand string word (pointed to by EDI) from the value of EAX. The result is not stored, but the flags are updated. Then the value of EDI changes in increments or decrements of 4, depending on the setting of the direction flag. Usually, this instruction is used with the REPE, REPNE, REPNZ, or REPZ instructions to repeat the scan for a maximum of CX bytes or until a match or difference is found.

Flags affected
OF, SF, ZF, AF, PF, CF

Coding examples
```
SCASD
REPNZ SCASD        ;Repeat a scan loop
```

SETA

Data-transfer

Set Byte if Above: SETA stores a 1 in the operand if the carry and zero flags both are clear. If this condition is not met, a 0 is stored in the operand. The operand must be a byte-length register or memory location. This instruction is functionally the same as SETNBE.

Coding example
```
SETA CL
```

SETAE

Data-transfer

Set Byte if Above or Equal: SETAE stores a 1 in the operand if the carry flag is clear. If this condition is not met, a 0 is stored in the operand. The operand must be a byte-length register or memory location. This instruction is functionally the same as SETNB or SETNC.

Coding example
```
SETAE CL
```

SETB

Data-transfer

Set Byte if Below: SETB stores a 1 in the operand if the carry flag is set. If this condition is not met, a 0 is stored in the operand. The operand must be a byte-length register or memory location. This instruction is functionally the same as SETC or SETNAE.

Coding example
```
SETB CL
```

SETBE

Data-transfer

Set Byte if Below or Equal: SETBE stores a 1 in the operand if either the carry or zero flag is set. If this condition is not met, a 0 is stored in the operand. The operand must be a byte-length register or memory location. This instruction is functionally the same as SETNA.

Coding example

```
SETBE CL
```

SETC

Data-transfer

Set Byte on Carry: SETC stores a 1 in the operand if the carry flag is set. If this condition is not met, a 0 is stored in the operand. The operand must be a byte-length register or memory location. This instruction is functionally the same as SETB or SETNAE.

Coding example

```
SETC CL
```

SETE

Data-transfer

Set Byte if Equal: SETE stores a 1 in the operand if the zero flag is set. If this condition is not met, a 0 is stored in the operand. The operand must be a byte-length register or memory location. This instruction is functionally the same as SETZ.

Coding example

```
SETE CL
```

SETG

Data-transfer

Set Byte if Greater: SETG stores a 1 in the operand if the sign flag equals the overflow flag or the zero flag is clear. If either condition is not met, a 0 is stored in the operand. The operand must be a byte-length register or memory location. This instruction is functionally the same as SETNLE.

Coding example

```
SETG CL
```

SETGE

Data-transfer

Set Byte if Greater or Equal: SETGE stores a 1 in the operand if the sign flag equals the overflow flag. If this condition is not met, a 0 is stored in the operand. The operand must be a byte-length register or memory location. This instruction is functionally the same as SETNL.

Coding example

```
SETGE CL
```

SETL

Data-transfer

Set Byte if Less Than: SETL stores a 1 in the operand if the sign flag does not equal the overflow flag. If this condition is not met, a 0 is stored in the operand. The operand must be a byte-length register or memory location. This instruction is functionally the same as SETNGE.

Coding example

```
SETL CL
```

SETLE

Data-transfer

Set Byte if Less Than or Equal: SETLE stores a 1 in the operand if the sign flag does not equal the overflow flag or the zero flag is set. If either condition is not met, a 0 is stored in the operand. The operand must be a byte-length register or memory location. This instruction is functionally the same as SETNG.

Coding example
```
SETLE CL
```

SETNA

Data-transfer

Set Byte if Not Above: SETNA stores a 1 in the operand if either the carry or zero flag is set. If either condition is not met, a 0 is stored in the operand. The operand must be a byte-length register or memory location. This instruction is functionally the same as SETBE.

Coding example
```
SETNA CL
```

SETNAE

Data-transfer

Set Byte if Not Above or Equal: SETNAE stores a 1 in the operand if the carry flag is set. If this condition is not met, a 0 is stored in the operand. The operand must be a byte-length register or memory location. This instruction is functionally the same as SETB or SETC.

Coding example
```
SETNAE CL
```

SETNB

Data-transfer

Set Byte if Not Below: SETNB stores a 1 in the operand if the carry flag is clear. If this condition is not met, a 0 is stored in the operand. The operand must be a byte-length register or memory location. This instruction is functionally the same as SETAE or SETNC.

Coding example
```
SETNB CL
```

SETNBE

Data-transfer

Set Byte if Not Below or Equal: SETNBE stores a 1 in the operand if both the carry and zero flags are clear. If this condition is not met, a 0 is stored in the operand. The operand must be a byte-length register or memory location. This instruction is functionally the same as SETA.

Coding example
```
SETNBE CL
```

SETNC

Data-transfer

Set Byte on No Carry: SETNC stores a 1 in the operand if the carry flag is clear. If this condition is not met, a 0 is stored in the operand. The operand must be a byte-length register or memory location. This instruction is functionally the same as SETAE or SETNB.

Coding example
```
SETNC CL
```

SETNE

Data-transfer

Set Byte if Not Equal: SETNE stores a 1 in the operand if the zero flag is clear. If this condition is not met, a 0 is stored in the operand. The operand must be a byte-length register or memory location. This instruction is functionally the same as SETNZ.

Coding example
```
SETNE CL
```

SETNG

Data-transfer

Set Byte if Not Greater Than: SETNG stores a 1 in the operand if the sign flag does not equal the overflow flag or the zero flag is set. If either condition is not met, a 0 is stored in the operand. The operand must be a byte-length register or memory location. This instruction is functionally the same as SETLE.

Coding example
```
SETNG CL
```

SETNGE

Data-transfer

Set Byte if Not Greater Than or Equal: SETNGE stores a 1 in the operand if the sign flag does not equal the overflow flag. If this condition is not met, a 0 is stored in the operand. The operand must be a byte-length register or memory location. This instruction is functionally the same as SETL.

Coding example
```
SETNGE CL
```

SETNL

Data-transfer

Set Byte if Not Less Than: SETNL stores a 1 in the operand if the sign flag equals the overflow flag. If this condition is not met, a 0 is stored in the operand. The operand must be a byte-length register or memory location. This instruction is functionally the same as SETGE.

Coding example
```
SETNL CL
```

SETNLE

Data-transfer

Set Byte if Not Less Than or Equal: SETNLE stores a 1 in the operand if the sign flag equals the overflow flag or the zero flag is clear. If either condition is not met, a 0 is stored in the operand. The operand must be a byte-length register or memory location. This instruction is functionally the same as SETG.

Coding example
```
SETNLE CL
```

SETNO

Data-transfer

Set Byte on No Overflow: SETNO stores a 1 in the operand if the overflow flag is clear. If this condition is not met, a 0 is stored in the operand. The operand must be a byte-length register or memory location.

Coding example
```
SETNO CL
```

SETNP

Data-transfer

Set Byte on No Parity: SETNP stores a 1 in the operand if the parity flag is clear. If this condition is not met, a 0 is stored in the operand. The operand must be a byte-length register or memory location. This instruction is functionally the same as SETPO.

Coding example
```
SETNP CL
```

SETNS

Data-transfer

Set Byte on Not Sign: SETNS stores a 1 in the operand if the sign flag is clear. If this condition is not met, a 0 is stored in the operand. The operand must be a byte-length register or memory location.

Coding example
```
SETNS CL
```

SETNZ

Data-transfer

Set Byte if Not Zero: SETNZ stores a 1 in the operand if the zero flag is clear. If this condition is not met, a 0 is stored in the operand. The operand must be a byte-length register or memory location. This instruction is functionally the same as SETNE.

Coding example
```
SETNZ CL
```

SETO

Data-transfer

Set Byte on Overflow: SETO stores a 1 in the operand if the overflow flag is set. If this condition is not met, a 0 is stored in the operand. The operand must be a byte-length register or memory location.

Coding example
```
SETO CL
```

SETP

Data-transfer

Set Byte on Parity: SETP stores a 1 in the operand if the parity flag is set. If this condition is not met, a 0 is stored in the operand. The operand must be a byte-length register or memory location. This instruction is functionally the same as SETPE.

Coding example
```
SETP CL
```

SETPE

Data-transfer

Set Byte on Parity Even: SETPE stores a 1 in the operand if the parity flag is set. If this condition is not met, a 0 is stored in the operand. The operand must be a byte-length register or memory location. This instruction is functionally the same as SETP.

Coding example
```
SETPE CL
```

SETPO

Data-transfer

Set Byte on Parity Odd: SETPO stores a 1 in the operand if the parity flag is clear. If this condition is not met, a 0 is stored in the operand. The operand must be a byte-length register or memory location. This instruction is functionally the same as SETNP.

Coding example

```
SETPO CL
```

SETS

Data-transfer

Set Byte on Sign: SETS stores a 1 in the operand if the sign flag is set. If this condition is not met, a 0 is stored in the operand. The operand must be a byte-length register or memory location.

Coding example

```
SETS CL
```

SETZ

Data-transfer

Set Byte if Zero: SETZ stores a 1 in the operand if the zero flag is set. If this condition is not met, a 0 is stored in the operand. The operand must be a byte-length register or memory location. This instruction is functionally the same as SETE.

Coding example

```
SETZ CL
```

SHL

Bit-manipulation

Shift Left: SHL shifts all bits in the destination operand to the left by the number of places specified in the source operand. High-order bits are lost, and low-order bits are cleared.

Flags affected
OF, SF, ZF, PF, CF, AF (undefined)

Coding examples
```
SHL EAX,1
SHL BL,3
SHL DX,16
SHL TEMP,CL
```

SHLD

Bit-manipulation

Shift Left, Double Precision: SHLD shifts all bits in the first operand to the left by the number of places specified in the third operand. High-order bits are lost, and low-order bits are copied from the second operand, starting with the second operand's low-order bit. The result is stored in the first operand.

Flags affected
SF, ZF, PF, CF, OF (undefined) AF (undefined)

Coding examples
```
SHLD AX,BX,4
SHLD DWORD_TEMP,EAX,16
```

SHR

Bit-manipulation

Shift Right: SHR shifts all bits in the destination operand to the right by the number of places specified in the source operand. Low-order bits are lost, and high-order bits are cleared.

Flags affected
OF, SF, ZF, PF, CF, AF (undefined)

Coding examples
```
SHR EAX,1
SHR BL,3
SHR DX,16
SHR TEMP,CL
```

SHRD

Bit-manipulation

Shift Right, Double Precision: SHRD shifts all bits in the first operand to the right by the number of places specified in the third operand. Low-order bits are lost, and high-order bits are copied from the second operand, starting with the second operand's high-order bit. The result is stored in the first operand.

Flags affected
SF, ZF, PF, CF, OF (undefined), AF (undefined)

Coding examples
```
SHRD AX,BX,4
SHRD DWORD_TEMP,EAX,16
```

STOSD

String-manipulation

Store Doubleword in EAX at String: This instruction copies the contents of EAX to the word address pointed to by EDI. DI then changes in increments or decrements of 4, depending on the setting of the direction flag.

SUB

Arithmetic

Subtract: SUB subtracts the contents of the source operand from (and stores the result in) the destination operand. In this instruction, the values being added are assumed to be binary.

Flags affected
OF, SF, ZF, AF, PF, CF

Coding examples
```
SUB  AX,BX          ;AX=AX-AX
SUB  AX,TEMP        ;AX=AX-TEMP
SUB  SUM,EBX        ;SUM=SUM-EBX
SUB  CL,10          ;CL=CL-10
SUB  AX,TEMP[BX]    ;Indirect address
```

TEST

Bit-manipulation

Test Bits: TEST performs a logical AND of the operands, but the result is not stored. Only the flags are affected. Each bit of the resultant byte or word is set to 1, only if the corresponding bit of each operand is 1.

Flags affected
OF, SF, ZF, PF, CF, AF (undefined)

Coding examples

```
TEST AX,BX          ;
TEST AX,TEMP        ;TEMP must be a word
TEST SUM,EBX        ;SUM must be a dword
TEST CL,00001111b;
TEST AX,TEMP[BX]    ;Indirect address
```

XCHG

Data-transfer

Exchange: Swaps contents of the source and destination operands. The length of both operands must agree.

Coding examples

```
XCHG AX,BX          ;Swap AX with BX
XCHG EAX,DWRD       ;Swap EAX with DWRD
XCHG CL,CH          ;Swap CL with CH
XCHG AX,TEMP        ;Swap AX with TEMP
```

XOR

Bit-manipulation

Logical Exclusive-Or on Bits: XOR performs a logical XOR of the operands and stores the result in the destination operand. Each bit of the resultant byte or word is set to 1, only if the corresponding bits of each operand contain opposite values.

Flags affected
OF, SF, ZF, PF, CF, AF (undefined)

Coding examples

```
XOR AX,BX           ;
XOR EAX,TEMP        ;TEMP must be a dword
XOR SUM,BX          ;SUM must be a word
XOR CL,00001111b    ;
XOR AX,TEMP[BX]     ;Indirect address
```

Intel Numeric Coprocessors

Three different numeric coprocessors are in the Intel series. These are the 8087 (which works with the 8086/8088), the 80287 (which works with the 80286 or 80386), and the 80387 (which works with the 80386). Intel calls these chips "numeric processor extensions" because, for all intents and purposes, they appear to be transparent to programmers. The instruction and register sets of the main microprocessors simply seem to be expanded.

As with the relationship between the 8086/8088 and successive generations of microprocessors, the base instruction set for the Intel numeric coprocessors is captured within the 8087. Later in this quick reference, the extensions to this base set (as embodied in later numeric coprocessors) are explored.

Before you begin looking at the register and instruction sets for any of the numeric coprocessors, you must realize that the 8087 works on the principle of a floating stack (similar to that of the 8086/8088), in which virtually all operations are performed.

The Stack Registers

The 8087 and 80287 use eight internal stack registers, each of which is 80 bits wide. These stack registers are numbered 0 through 7, with most operations capable of addressing these registers directly as ST, ST(1), ST(2), ST(3), and so on, through ST(7).

The 8087 Status Word

The 8087 uses a status word to describe the current condition of the 8087. The following list shows the codes for the status word flags and the meaning of each code:

Code	Use
IE	Invalid operation exception
DE	Denormalized operand exception
ZE	Zerodivide exception
OE	Overflow exception
UE	Underflow exception
PE	Precision exception
IR	Interrupt request
C0	Condition code 0
C1	Condition code 1
C2	Condition code 2
ST	Stack-top pointer
C3	Condition code 3
B	Busy signal

This status word cannot be examined directly. It must be transferred by specific 8087 instructions to memory, where it can be analyzed by 8086/8088 instructions.

The 8087 Control Word

The 8087 uses a control word for program control of the 8087 operations. The flags (or status codes) of this 16-bit word are detailed as follows:

Code	Use
IM	Invalid operation exception mask
DM	Denormalized operand exception mask
ZM	Zerodivide exception mask
OM	Overflow exception mask
UM	Underflow exception mask
PM	Precision exception mask
IEM	Interrupt enable mask
	0 = Interrupts enabled
	1 = Interrupts disabled
PC	Precision control
	00 = 24 bits
	01 = (Reserved)
	10 = 53 bits
	11 = 64 bits

Code	Use
RC	Rounding control
	00 = Round to nearest or even
	01 = Round down
	10 = Round up
	11 = Truncate
IC	Infinity control
	0 = Projective
	1 = Affine

This word can be constructed in the main memory and then directed to the 8087 by specific 8087 instructions.

Later numeric coprocessors have altered this control word slightly; the differences are covered later in this quick reference.

Instruction Set Groupings

The 8087 extends, by 77 instructions, the instruction set of the 8086/8088. This section details only those 77 instructions, grouped according to the purpose of the instruction. The six general classifications of instructions are

> Data transfer
> Arithmetic
> Comparisons
> Transcendental
> Constant
> Processor control

Overview of the Intel 8087

The following list shows the instructions available with the 8087:

F2XM1	FBSTP	FCOMPP
FABS	FCHS	FDECSTP
FADD	FCLEX	FDISI
FADDP	FCOM	FDIV
FBLD	FCOMP	FDIVP

FDIVR	FLDL2E	FRSTOR
FDIVRP	FLDL2T	FSAVE
FENI	FLDLG2	FSCALE
FFREE	FLDLN2	FSQRT
FIADD	FLDPI	FST
FICOM	FLDZ	FSTCW
FICOMP	FMUL	FSTENV
FIDIV	FMULP	FSTP
FIDIVR	FNCLEX	FSTSW
FILD	FNDISI	FSUB
FIMUL	FNENI	FSUBP
FINCSTP	FNINIT	FSUBR
FINIT	FNOP	FSUBRP
FIST	FNSAVE	FTST
FISTP	FNSTCW	FWAIT
FISUB	FNSTENV	FXAM
FISUBR	FNSTSW	FXCH
FLD	FPATAN	FXTRACT
FLD1	FPREM	FYL2X
FLDCW	FPTAN	FYL2XP1
FLDENV	FRNDINT	

The following list of the 8087 instruction set is arranged by general instruction classification. The instructions listed within each classification are in alphabetical order.

Arithmetic

FABS	FISUB	*Comparison*
FADD	FISUBR	FCOM
FADDP	FMUL	FCOMP
FCHS	FMULP	FCOMPP
FDIV	FPREM	FICOM
FDIVP	FRNDINT	FICOMP
FDIVR	FSCALE	FTST
FDIVRP	FSQRT	FXAM
FIADD	FSUB	
FIDIV	FSUBP	*Constant*
FIDIVR	FSUBR	FLD1
FIMUL	FSUBRP	FLDL2E
	FXTRACT	FLDL2T

FLDLG2	*Processor-*	FNSTCW
FLDLN2	*control*	FNSTENV
FLDPI	FCLEX	FNSTSW
FLDZ	FDECSTP	FRSTOR
	FDISI	FSAVE
Data-	FENI	FSTCW
transfer	FFREE	FSTENV
FBLD	FINCSTP	FSTSW
FBSTP	FINIT	FWAIT
FILD	FLDCW	
FIST	FLDENV	*Transcen-*
FISTP	FNCLEX	*dental*
FLD	FNDISI	F2XM1
FST	FNENI	FPATAN
FSTP	FNINIT	FPTAN
FXCH	FNOP	FYL2X
	FNSAVE	FYL2XP1

The following table shows how the 8087 instructions affect numeric-coprocessor status flags. An *X* in a column indicates that the status flag is changed by the instruction; a question mark indicates that the status flag is undefined after the instruction is executed. Only those instructions that affect status are included in this table.

Inst.	_B_	_C3_	_ST_	_C2_	_C1_	_C0_	_IR_	_PE_	_UE_	_OE_	_ZE_	_DE_	_IE_
F2XM1								X	X				
FABS													X
FADD								X	X	X		X	X
FADDP								X	X	X		X	X
FBLD													X
FBSTP													X
FCHS													X
FCLEX	X						X	X	X	X	X	X	X
FCOM		X		X	X							X	X
FCOMP		X		X	X							X	X
FCOMPP		X		X	X							X	X
FDECSTP			X										
FDIV								X	X	X	X	X	X
FDIVP								X	X	X	X	X	X

Inst.	B	C3	ST	C2	C1	C0	IR	PE	UE	OE	ZE	DE	IE
FDIVR								X	X	X	X	X	X
FDIVRP								X	X	X	X	X	X
FIADD								X		X		X	X
FICOM		X		X		X						X	X
FICOMP		X		X		X						X	X
FIDIV								X	X	X	X	X	X
FIDIVR								X	X	X	X	X	X
FILD													X
FIMUL								X		X		X	X
FINCSTP			X										
FIST								X					X
FISTP								X					X
FISUB								X		X		X	X
FISUBR								X		X		X	X
FLD												X	X
FLD1													X
FLDENV	X	X	X	X	X	X	X	X	X	X	X	X	X
FLDL2E													X
FLDL2T													X
FLDLG2													X
FLDLN2													X
FLDPI													X
FLDZ													X
FMUL								X	X	X		X	X
FMULP								X	X	X		X	X
FNCLEX	X						X	X	X	X	X	X	X
FPATAN								X	X				
FPREM		X			X	X			X			X	X
FPTAN								X					X
FRNDINT								X					X
FRSTOR	X	X	X	X	X	X	X	X	X	X	X	X	X
FSCALE									X	X			X
FSQRT								X				X	X
FST								X	X	X			X
FSTP								X	X	X			X
FSUB								X	X	X		X	X
FSUBP								X	X	X		X	X
FSUBR								X	X	X		X	X
FSUBRP								X	X	X		X	X
FTST		X		X		X						X	X

Inst.	B	C3	ST	C2	C1	C0	IR	PE	UE	OE	ZE	DE	IE
FXAM		X		X	X	X							
FXCH													X
FXTRACT											X		
FYL2X						X							
FYL2XP1					X								

Instruction Set for the Intel 8087

The balance of this section is designed as a reference to
the 8087 instruction set. Each instruction is described
in ascending numerical order. The following information is listed for each instruction:

Instruction name. This name is based on the standard
mnemonic code designed by Intel. The general classification for the instruction is provided also, along with a
narrative description of the instruction.

Status affected. The majority of the instructions change
the status word in one way or another. If the status
word is not affected, this category is not included for
the instruction.

Coding examples. Brief examples of the use of the
instruction are given. An example is included only if
the instruction name is not used alone; that is, operands
or additional instructions are needed to make the
instruction work.

=F2XM1

Transcendental

2x-1: Calculates $Y=2^x-1$, where X is the top stack
element (ST). The result (Y) replaces X as the top stack
element (ST). This instruction performs no validation
checking of the input value. The program ensures that
$0<=X<=0.5$.

Status affected
PE, UE

FABS

Arithmetic

Absolute Value: Changes the top stack element (ST) to
its absolute value.

Status affected
IE

FADD

Arithmetic

Add Real: Adds two numbers together and stores them
at the destination operand. If no destination operand is
given (only one operand is specified), ST is assumed to
be the destination.

Status affected
PE, UE, OE, DE, IE

Coding examples
```
FADD TEMP          ; ST=ST+TEMP
FADD TEMP,ST(3)    ; TEMP=TEMP+ST(3)
```

FADDP

Arithmetic

Add Real and Pop: Adds two numbers together, stores
them at the destination operand, and pops the stack. If
no destination operand is given (only one operand is
specified), ST is assumed to be the destination.

Coding examples
```
FADDP  TEMP        ; ST=ST+TEMP
FADDP  TEMP,ST(3)  ; TEMP=TEMP+ST(3)
```

FBLD   *Data-transfer*

BCD Load: Converts the BCD number at the operand address to a temporary real and pushes on the stack.

Status affected
    IE

Coding example
```
FBLD  TEMP
```

FBSTP   *Data-transfer*

BCD Store and Pop: Converts the top stack element (ST) to a BCD integer, stores it at the operand address, and pops the stack.

Status affected
    IE

Coding example
```
FBSTP  TEMP
```

FCHS

Arithmetic

Change Sign: Changes the sign of the top stack element (ST).

Status affected
    IE

FCLEX

Processor-control

Clear Exceptions with WAIT: Clears the exception flags, interrupt request, and busy flags of the 8087 status word. This instruction is preceded by a CPU wait prefix. See also FNCLEX.

Status affected
    B, IR, PE, UE, OE, ZE, DE, IE

FCOM

Comparison

Compare Real: The top stack element (ST) is compared to either the second stack element (ST(1)) or another specified operand. Condition codes are affected accordingly.

Status affected
    C3, C2, C0, DE, IE

Coding examples
```
FCOM                    ;Compare ST to ST(1)
FCOM ST(4)              ;Compare ST to ST(4)
FCOM TEMP               ;Compare ST to memory
```

FCOMP

Comparison

Compare Real and Pop: The top stack element (ST) is compared to either the second stack element (ST(1)) or another specified operand; the stack then is popped. Condition codes are affected accordingly.

Status affected
C3, C2, C0, DE, IE

Coding examples

```
FCOMP              ;Compare ST to ST(1)
FCOMP ST(4)        ;Compare ST to ST(4)
FCOMP TEMP         ;Compare ST to memory
```

FCOMPP

Comparison

Compare Real and Pop Twice: The top stack element (ST) is compared to the second stack element (ST(1)) and the stack is popped twice. Condition codes are affected accordingly.

Status affected
C3, C2, C0, DE, IE

FDECSTP

Processor-control

Decrement Stack Pointer: Decrements the stack pointer of the 8087 status word.

Status affected
ST

FDISI

Processor-control

Disable Interrupts with WAIT: Sets the interrupt enable mask of the 8087 control word, thus preventing the 8087 from initiating an interrupt. This instruction is preceded by a CPU wait prefix. See also FNDISI.

FDIV

Arithmetic

Divide Real: Divides the destination by the source operand, and stores the result at the destination operand. If no destination operand is given (only one operand is specified), ST is assumed to be the destination.

Status affected
PE, UE, OE, ZE, DE, IE

Coding examples
```
FDIV TEMP            ; ST=TEMP/ST
FDIV TEMP,ST(3)      ; TEMP=ST(3)/TEMP
```

FDIVP

Arithmetic

Divide Real and Pop: Divides the destination by the source operand, stores the result at the destination operand, and pops the stack. If no destination operand is given (only one operand is specified), ST is assumed to be the destination.

Status affected
PE, UE, OE, ZE, DE, IE

Coding examples
```
FDIVP TEMP          ; ST=TEMP/ST
FDIVP TEMP,ST(3)    ; TEMP=ST(3)/TEMP
```

FDIVR
Arithmetic

Divide Real Reversed: Divides the source by the destination operand, and stores the result at the destination operand. If no destination operand is given (only one operand is specified), ST is assumed to be the destination.

Status affected
PE, UE, OE, ZE, DE, IE

Coding examples
```
FDIVR TEMP          ; ST=ST/TEMP
FDIVR TEMP,ST(3)    ; TEMP=TEMP/ST(3)
```

FDIVRP
Arithmetic

Divide Real Reversed and Pop: Divides the source by the destination operand, stores the result at the destination operand, and pops the stack. If no destination operand is given (only one operand is specified), ST is assumed to be the destination.

Status affected
PE, UE, OE, ZE, DE, IE

Coding examples
```
FDIVRP TEMP         ; ST=ST/TEMP
FDIVRP TEMP,ST(3)   ; TEMP=TEMP/ST(3)
```

FENI

Processor-control

Enable Interrupts with WAIT: Clears the interrupt enable mask of the 8087 control word, thus allowing the 8087 to initiate interrupts. This instruction is preceded by a CPU wait prefix. See also FNENI.

FFREE

Processor-control

Free Register: Changes the tag for the specified stack register to indicate that the stack register is empty.

Coding example
```
FFREE ST(3)
```

FIADD

Arithmetic

Integer Add: Adds two numbers together as integers and stores them at the destination operand. If no destination operand is given (only one operand is specified), ST is assumed to be the destination.

Status affected
PE, OE, DE, IE

Coding examples
```
FIADD TEMP          ; ST=ST+TEMP
FIADD TEMP,ST(3)    ; TEMP=TEMP+ST(3)
```

FICOM

Comparison

Integer Compare: Converts the operand (assumed to be an integer) to a temporary real and compares it to the top stack element (ST). Condition codes are set accordingly.

Status affected
C3, C2, C0, DE, IE

Coding example
```
FICOM TEMP_INT    ;Compare memory to ST
```

FICOMP

Comparison

Integer Compare and Pop: Converts the operand (assumed to be an integer) to a temporary real, compares it to the top stack element (ST), and then pops the stack. Condition codes are set accordingly.

Status affected
C3, C2, C0, DE, IE

Coding example
```
FICOMP TEMP_INT   ;Compare memory to ST
```

FIDIV

Arithmetic

Integer Divide: Divides the destination by the source operand, as integers, and stores the result at the destination operand. If no destination operand is given (only one operand is specified), ST is assumed to be the destination.

Status affected
    PE, UE, OE, ZE, DE, IE

Coding examples
```
FIDIV TEMP          ; ST=TEMP/ST
FIDIV TEMP,ST(3)    ; TEMP=ST(3)/TEMP
```

FIDIVR

Arithmetic

Integer Divide Reversed: Divides the source by the destination operand, as integers, and stores the result at the destination operand. If no destination operand is given (only one operand is specified), ST is assumed to be the destination.

Status affected
    PE, UE, OE, ZE, DE, IE

Coding examples
```
FIDIVR TEMP          ; ST=ST/TEMP
FIDIVR TEMP,ST(3)    ; TEMP=TEMP/ST(3)
```

FILD

Data-transfer

Integer Load: Converts the binary integer number at the operand address to a temporary real, and pushes it on the stack.

Status affected
    IE

Coding example
```
FILD TEMP
```

FIMUL

Arithmetic

Integer Multiply: Multiplies the source by the destination operand, as integers, and stores the result at the destination operand. If no destination operand is given (only one operand is specified), ST is assumed to be the destination.

Status affected
PE, OE, DE, IE

Coding examples
```
FIMUL TEMP          ; ST=ST*TEMP
FIMUL TEMP,ST(3)    ; TEMP=TEMP*ST(3)
```

FINCSTP

Processor-control

Increment Stack Pointer: Increments the stack pointer of the 8087 status word.

Status affected
ST

FINIT

Processor-control

Initialize Processor with WAIT: Initializes the 8087. This action is functionally equivalent to performing a hardware RESET. This instruction is preceded by a CPU wait prefix. See also FNINIT.

FIST

Data-transfer

Integer Store: Rounds the top stack element (ST) to a binary integer number, and stores it at the operand address.

Status affected
PE, IE

Coding example
    FIST TEMP

FISTP

Data-transfer

Integer Store and Pop: Rounds the top stack element (ST) to a binary integer number, stores it at the operand address, and pops ST from the stack.

Status affected
PE, IE

Coding example
    FIST TEMP

FISUB

Arithmetic

Integer Subtract: Subtracts the source from the destination operand, as integers, and stores the result at the destination operand. If no destination operand is given (only one operand is specified), ST is assumed to be the destination.

Status affected
      PE, OE, DE, IE

Coding examples
```
FISUB TEMP          ; ST=ST-TEMP
FISUB TEMP,ST(3)  ; TEMP=TEMP-ST(3)
```

FISUBR

Arithmetic

Integer Subtract Reversed: Subtracts the destination
from the source operand, as integers, and stores the
result at the destination operand. If no destination
operand is given (only one operand is specified), ST is
assumed to be the destination.

Status affected
      PE, OE, DE, IE

Coding examples
```
FISUBR TEMP          ; ST=TEMP-ST
FISUBR TEMP,ST(3) ; TEMP=ST(3)-TEMP
```

FLD

Data-transfer

Load Real: Pushes the value of the source operand on
the stack.

Status affected
      DE, IE

Coding examples
```
FLD ST(3)
FLD TEMP
```

FLD1
Constant

Load 1.0: Pushes the value +1.0 on the stack. This value becomes ST.

Status affected
IE

FLDCW
Processor-control

Load Control Word: Loads the 8087 control word with the word value pointed to by the source operand.

Coding example
```
FLDCW MEM_CW    ;Transfer control word
```

FLDENV
Processor-control

Load Environment: Restores all environment variables of the 8087 from the 14-word memory location specified by the operand.

Status affected
B, C3, ST, C2, C1, C0, IR, PE, UE, OE, ZE, DE, IE

Coding example
```
FLDENV SAVE_AREA
```

Constant

Load $\log_2 e$: Pushes the value of $LOG_2 e$ on the stack.
This value becomes ST.

_____
Status affected
IE

Constant

Load $\log_2 10$: Pushes the value of $LOG_2 10$ on the stack.
This value becomes ST.

_____
Status affected
IE

Constant

Load $\log_{10} 2$: Pushes the value of $LOG_{10} 2$ on the stack.
This value becomes ST.

_____
Status affected
IE

FLDLN2

Constant

Load $\log_e 2$: Pushes the value of $LOG_e 2$ on the stack.
This value becomes ST.

_____
Status affected
IE

FLDPI

Constant

Load Pi: Pushes the value of pi on the stack. This value becomes ST.

Status affected
IE

FLDZ

Constant

Load 0.0: Pushes the value 0.0 on the stack. This value becomes ST.

Status affected
IE

FMUL

Arithmetic

Multiply Real: Multiplies the source by the destination operand, and stores the result at the destination operand. If no destination operand is given (only one operand is specified), ST is assumed to be the destination.

Status affected
PE, UE, OE, DE, IE

Coding examples
```
FMUL  TEMP          ; ST=ST*TEMP
FMUL  TEMP,ST(3)    ; TEMP=TEMP*ST(3)
```

FMULP

Arithmetic

Multiply Real and Pop: Multiplies the source by the destination operand, stores the result at the destination operand, and pops the stack. If no destination operand is given (only one operand is specified), ST is assumed to be the destination.

Status affected
PE, UE, OE, DE, IE

Coding examples
```
FMULP  TEMP         ; ST=ST*TEMP
FMULP  TEMP,ST(3)   ; TEMP=TEMP*ST(3)
```

FNCLEX

Processor-control

Clear Exceptions: Clears the exception flags, interrupt request, and busy flags of the 8087 status word. This instruction is not preceded by a CPU wait prefix. See also FCLEX.

Status affected
B, IR, PE, UE, OE, ZE, DE, IE

FNDISI

Processor-control

Disable Interrupts: Sets the interrupt enable mask of the 8087 control word, thus preventing the 8087 from initiating an interrupt. This instruction is not preceded by a CPU wait prefix. See also FDISI.

FNENI

Processor-control

Enable Interrupts: Clears the interrupt enable mask of the 8087 control word, thus allowing the 8087 to initiate interrupts. This instruction is not preceded by a CPU wait prefix. See also FENI.

FNINIT

Processor-control

Initialize Processor: Initializes the 8087. This action is functionally equivalent to performing a hardware RESET. This instruction is not preceded by a CPU wait prefix. See also FINIT.

FNOP

Processor-control

No Operation: Does nothing but take time and space— the 8087 performs no operation.

FNSAVE

Processor-control

Save State: Saves, at the memory location specified by the operand, all registers and environment variables of the 8087. This save requires 94 words of memory. After the save, the 8087 is initialized as though the FINIT or FNINIT instructions had been issued. This instruction (FNSAVE) is not preceded by a CPU wait prefix. See also FSAVE.

Coding example
```
FNSAVE SAVE_AREA
```

FNSTCW

Processor-control

Store Control Word: Copies the 8087 control word to the word value pointed to by the source operand. This instruction is not preceded by a CPU wait prefix. See also FSTCW.

Coding example
```
FNSTCW MEM_CW   ;Transfer control word
```

FNSTENV

Processor-control

Store Environment: Saves, at the memory location specified by the operand, all environment variables of the 8087. This save requires 14 words of memory. After the save, this instruction sets the exception masks of the 8087 control word. This instruction is not preceded by a CPU wait prefix. See also FSTENV.

Coding example
```
FNSTENV SAVE_AREA
```

FNSTSW

Processor-control

Store Status Word: Copies the 8087 status word to the word value pointed to by the source operand. This instruction is not preceded by a CPU wait prefix. See also FSTSW.

Coding example

```
FNSTSW MEM_SW     ;Transfer status word
```

FPATAN

Transcendental

Partial Arctangent: Computes q=ARCTAN(Y/X), where X is the top stack element (ST) and Y is the second stack element (ST(1)). Both stack elements are popped, and the result (0) is pushed on the stack and becomes ST. This instruction performs no validation checking of the input value. The program ensures that $0<Y<X<\infty$.

Status affected

PE, UE

FPREM

Arithmetic

Partial Remainder: Calculates the modulo of the two top stack elements. By successively subtracting ST(1) from ST, an exact remainder is calculated and remains in ST.

Status affected

C3, C1, C0, UE, DE, IE

FPTAN

Transcendental

Partial Tangent: Computes Y/X=TAN(Z), where Z is
the top stack element (ST). The top stack element is
replaced by the computed Y, and the computed X is
pushed on the stack. Thus, at the end of this operation,
ST(1)=Y and ST=X. This instruction performs no
validation checking of the input value.

Status affected
    PE, IE

FRNDINT

Arithmetic

Round to Integer: Rounds the number in the top stack
element (ST) to an integer.

Status affected
    PE, IE

FRSTOR

Processor-control

Restore State: Restores all registers and environment
variables of the 8087 from the 94-word memory
location specified by the operand.

Status affected
    B, C3, ST, C2, C1, C0, IR, PE, UE, OE, ZE, DE, IE

Coding example
    FRSTOR SAVE_AREA

FSAVE

Processor-control

Save State with WAIT: Saves, at the memory location specified by the operand, all registers and environment variables of the 8087. This save requires 94 words of memory. After the save, the 8087 is initialized as though the FINIT or FNINIT instructions had been issued. This instruction (FSAVE) is preceded by a CPU wait prefix. See also FNSAVE.

Coding example
```
FSAVE SAVE_AREA
```

FSCALE

Arithmetic

Scale: Calculates $X=X*2^Y$, where X is the value of the top stack element (ST), and Y is the value of the second stack element (ST(1)).

Status affected
UE, OE, IE

FSQRT

Arithmetic

Square Root: Calculates the square root of the top stack element (ST) and stores it as the new ST. The old ST is lost.

Status affected
PE, DE, IE

FST

Data-transfer

Store Real: Copies the value of the top stack element (ST) to the operand or operand address.

Status affected
PE, UE, OE, IE

Coding examples
```
FST  ST(3)
FST  TEMP
```

FSTCW

Processor-control

Store Control Word with WAIT: Copies the 8087 control word to the word value pointed to by the source operand. This instruction is preceded by a CPU wait prefix. See also FNSTCW.

Coding example
```
FSTCW MEM_CW    ;Transfer control word
```

FSTENV

Processor-control

Store Environment with WAIT: Saves, at the memory location specified by the operand, all environment variables of the 8087. This save requires 14 words of memory. After the save, this instruction sets the exception masks of the 8087 control word. This instruction is preceded by a CPU wait prefix. See also FNSTENV.

Coding example
```
FSTENV SAVE_AREA
```

FSTP

Data-transfer

Store Real and Pop: Copies the value of the top stack element (ST) to the operand or operand address, and pops the stack.

Status affected
PE, UE, OE, IE

Coding examples
```
FSTP ST(3)
FSTP TEMP
```

FSTSW

Processor-control

Store Status Word with WAIT: Copies the 8087 status word to the word value pointed to by the source operand. This instruction is preceded by a CPU wait prefix. See also FNSTSW.

Coding example
```
FSTSW MEM_SW          ;Transfer status word
```

FSUB

Arithmetic

Subtract Real: Subtracts the source from the destination operand and stores the result at the destination operand. If no destination operand is given (only one operand is specified), ST is assumed to be the destination.

Status affected
PE, UE, OE, DE, IE

Coding examples
```
FSUB   TEMP          ; ST=ST-TEMP
FSUB   TEMP,ST(3)    ; TEMP=TEMP-ST(3)
```

FSUB P

Arithmetic

Subtract Real and Pop: Subtracts the source from the destination operand, stores the result at the destination operand, and pops the stack. If no destination operand is given (only one operand is specified), ST is assumed to be the destination.

Status affected
PE, UE, OE, DE, IE

Coding examples
```
FSUBP  TEMP          ; ST=ST-TEMP
FSUBP  TEMP,ST(3)    ; TEMP=TEMP-ST(3)
```

FSUBR

Arithmetic

Subtract Real Reversed: Subtracts the destination from the source operand and stores the result at the destination operand. If no destination operand is given (only one operand is specified), ST is assumed to be the destination.

Status affected
PE, UE, OE, DE, IE

Coding examples

```
FSUBR TEMP        ; ST=TEMP-ST
FSUBR TEMP,ST(3)  ; TEMP=ST(3)-TEMP
```

FSUBRP

Arithmetic

Subtract Real Reversed and Pop: Subtracts the destination from the source operand, stores the result at the destination operand, and pops the stack. If no destination operand is given (only one operand is specified), ST is assumed to be the destination.

Status affected

PE, UE, OE, DE, IE

Coding examples

```
FSUBRP TEMP        ; ST=TEMP-ST
FSUBRP TEMP,ST(3)  ; TEMP=ST(3)-TEMP
```

FTST

Comparison

Test: Compares the top stack element (ST) to zero and sets the condition codes accordingly.

Status affected

C3, C2, C0, DE, IE

FWAIT

Processor-control

CPU Wait: Effectively the same as the 8086/8088 WAIT command. This instruction permits the synchronization of the microprocessor and the numeric

coprocessor. It causes the microprocessor to suspend
operation until reception of a signal which indicates
that the numeric coprocessor has completed the last
operation.

FXAM

Comparison

Examine: Examines the top stack element (ST) and
reports (in the condition codes) the condition, or
attributes, of the value.

Status affected
C3, C2, C1, C0

FXCH

Data-transfer

Exchange Registers: Switches the value of the top stack
element (ST) with that of the operand.

Status affected
IE

Coding examples
```
FXCH ST(3)
FXCH TEMP
```

FXTRACT

Arithmetic

Extract Exponent and Significand: Removes the top
stack element (ST) and converts it to two numbers—the
exponent and significand of the original number. The

exponent is pushed on the stack, followed by the significand, which results in ST=significand and ST(1)=exponent.

Status affected
  IE

FYL2X

Transcendental

$Y*log_2X$: Calculates $Z=Y*LOG_2X$, where X is the top stack element (ST) and Y is the second stack element (ST(1)). Both stack elements are popped, and the result (Z) is pushed on the stack and becomes the new ST. This instruction performs no validation checking of the input value.

Status affected
  PE

FYL2XP1

Transcendental

$Y*log_2(X+1)$: Calculates $Z=Y*LOG_2(X=1)$, where X is the top stack element (ST) and Y is the second stack element (ST(1)). Both stack elements are popped, and the result (Z) is pushed on the stack and becomes the new ST. This instruction performs no validation checking of the input value.

Status affected
  PE

Instruction Set for the Intel 80287

A descendant of the 8087, the 80287 is similar in function to the 8087. Most instructions that work on the 8087 work correctly also on the 80287. Changes to the instruction set include the deletion of several processor-control instructions and the addition of a new processor-control instruction (FSETPM).

Several 8087 instructions (FDISI, FENI, FNDISI, and FNENI) have no counterpart in the instruction set of the 80287. Although programs for the 80287 should avoid these instructions, using the instructions does not cause problems on the 80287—the 80287 treats these instructions as "NOP" values, and no operation occurs.

Control and Status Word Differences

Earlier, this book mentioned that there is a difference between the status word of the 8087 and the 80287. The only difference is that the 80287 status word does not contain the IR (interrupt request) flag. The control word for the 80287 also has only one difference from that of the 8087: the IEM (interrupt enable mask) is missing.

══ FSETPM

Processor-control

Set Protected Mode: Causes the 80287 to operate in protected mode. Normally, the operation mode is of no concern to programmers of applications software.

Overview of the Intel 80387

Intel's third-generation numeric coprocessor, the 80387, is upwardly compatible with the 80287—and thus, with the 8087. As a descendant of the 8087 and 80287, the 80387 runs software designed for the earlier chips. The primary differences are in additional instructions, speed, and differences in the control and status words.

The 80387 extends by nine instructions the instruction set understood by the 80287. The same instruction-set grouping categories are maintained.

Control and Status Word Differences

Minor differences exist between the 80387 status word and that of its predecessors. The 80387 uses the same status word, except that the following status word flags are added:

Code	*Use*
SF	Stack fault
ES	Error summary status

The control word is essentially the same as that used by the 80287, with the exception that the infinity control flag has no meaning in the 80387. If your program uses the infinity control flag, there is no effect on the 80387; the bit is ignored.

80387 Instruction Set

The Intel 80387 instruction set is an extension of the instruction set for the 80287. Nine additional instructions are available, as follows:

FCOS	FSTSW AX
FNSTSW AX	FUCOM
FPREM1	FUCOMP
FSIN	FUCOMPP
FSINCOS	

The nine additional instructions for the Intel 80387, arranged by general instruction classification, are shown in the following list; within each classification, instructions are listed in alphabetical order:

Arithmetic	*Processor-control*
FPREM1	FNSTSW AX
	FSTSW AX
Comparison	
FUCOM	*Transcendental*
FUCOMP	FCOS
FUCOMPP	FSIN
	FSINCOS

The following table details how the 80387 instructions affect numeric-coprocessor status flags. An *X* in a column indicates that the status flag is changed by the instruction; a question mark indicates that the status flag is undefined after the instruction is executed. Only those instructions that affect status are included in this table.

Inst.	B	C3	ST	C2	C1	C0	IR	PE	UE	OE	ZE	DE	IE
FCOS								X	X			X	X
FPREM1	X		X	X	X				X			X	X
FSIN								X	X			X	X
FSINCOS								X	X			X	X
FUCOM	X	X	X									X	X
FUCOMP	X	X	X									X	X
FUCOMPP	X	X	X									X	X

Instruction Set for the Intel 80387

FCOS

Transcendental

Cosine: Computes the cosine of the top stack element (ST), which should be a number greater than or equal to 0, but less than 2^{63}. This number (expected to be in radians) is popped from the stack, and the result is pushed back on the stack.

Status affected
PE, UE, DE, IE

FNSTSW AX

Processor-control

Store Status Word: Copies the 80387 status word to the AX register of the 80386. The previous contents of the AX register are lost. This instruction is not preceded by a CPU wait prefix. See also FSTSW AX.

Coding example
```
FNSTSW AX          ;AX = status word
```

FPREM1

Arithmetic

Partial Remainder, IEEE compatible: Calculates the modulo of the two top stack elements. By successively subtracting ST(1) from ST, an exact remainder is calculated and remains in ST. See also FPREM.

Status affected
        C3, C2, C1, C0, UE, DE, IE

= FSIN

Transcendental

Sine: Computes the sine of the top stack element (ST), which should be a number greater than or equal to 0, but less than 2^{63}. This number (expected to be in radians) is popped from the stack and the result is pushed back on the stack.

Status affected
        PE, UE, DE, IE

= FSINCOS

Transcendental

Compute Sine, Then Cosine: Computes the sine of the top stack element (ST), which should be a number greater than or equal to 0, but less than 2^{63}. This number (expected to be in radians) is popped from the stack, and the result is pushed back on the stack. Then the cosine of the original ST value is computed and pushed on the stack. Thus, ST contains the cosine and ST(1) contains the sine at the completion of this instruction.

Status affected
        PE, UE, DE, IE

FSTSW AX

Processor-control

Store Status Word with WAIT: Copies the 80387 status word to the AX register of the 80386. The previous contents of the AX register are lost. This instruction is preceded by a CPU wait prefix. See also FNSTSW AX.

Coding example
```
FSTSW AX              ;AX = status word
```

FUCOM

Comparison

Compare Real: The top stack element (ST) is compared to either the second stack element (ST(1)) or another specified operand that also must exist as a stack element. Condition codes are affected accordingly. See also FCOM.

Status affected
C3, C2, C0, DE, IE

Coding examples
```
FUCOM                 ;Compare ST to ST(1)
FUCOM ST(4)           ;Compare ST to ST(4)
```

FUCOMP

Comparison

Compare Real and Pop: The top stack element (ST) is compared to either the second stack element (ST(1)) or another specified operand that also must exist as a stack element. The stack then is popped. Condition codes are affected accordingly. See also FCOMP.

Status affected

C3, C2, C0, DE, IE

Coding examples

```
FUCOMP                 ;Compare ST to ST(1)
FUCOMP ST(4)           ;Compare ST to ST(4)
```

FUCOMPP

Comparison

Compare Real and Pop Twice: The top stack element
(ST) is compared to the second stack element (ST(1)),
and the stack is popped twice. Condition codes are
affected accordingly. FUCOMPP differs from
FCOMPP in that IE is not set if one of the operands is
not a valid number.

Status affected

C3, C2, C0, DE, IE

Index